BEARING

Remaining

FRUIT

VOLUME ONE

WITNESS LEE

Living Stream Ministry

Anaheim, CA • www.lsm.org

© 2004 Living Stream Ministry

First Edition, February 2004.

ISBN 0-7363-2440-2 (2 volume set)
ISBN 0-7363-2438-0 (volume 1)

Published by

Living Stream Ministry
2431 W. La Palma Ave., Anaheim, CA 92801 U.S.A.
P. O. Box 2121, Anaheim, CA 92814 U.S.A.

Printed in the United States of America
04   05   06   07   08   09   10   /   9   8   7   6   5   4   3   2   1

CONTENTS

PREFACE

This book is composed of messages given by Brother Witness Lee to the full-time trainees in Taipei, Taiwan from January through May of 1987. The entire book contains twenty-nine chapters, divided into two volumes.

CHAPTER ONE

THE KEY TO THE SUCCESS
OF THE NEW WAY

THE EFFECT OF THE NEW WAY

In October of 1984, the church in Taipei began to change the system, and there was a scene of newness replacing the old, particularly regarding the method of our work, the church meetings, and the service. Not only was there a change in appearance outwardly, but even more there was a change inwardly, in the intrinsic nature. One year later it reached a certain scale. Then after another half year, in order to meet the need, we officially began the Full-time Training and the practice of going out to knock on doors, bringing people to be saved, and baptizing them. This was the first step of the new way.

In 1986 we baptized 7,100 people within one hundred days, and about a month later we baptized more than 1,100 people, totaling over 8,200. This figure is a proof that this new way is indeed effective. One brother from the United States testified that within those one hundred days he baptized one hundred twenty-nine persons, a brother from Malaysia said that he baptized one hundred twenty persons, and a brother from Anaheim said that he baptized over eighty persons.

THE EXAMPLES
OF SUCCESSFUL DOOR-KNOCKING
IN THE NEW WAY

In recent years, therefore, wherever there are churches in the Lord's recovery throughout the earth, localities have responded to this move of door-knocking, bringing people to be saved, and baptizing them. Regrettably, though, no one has fully known how to do these things. In the initial stage of the Full-time Training, all the practices in the training were not publicized. Because this training was for the most part in the experimental stage, without our firm assurance, we were reluctant to spread these unconfirmed results. We feared that once they were spread, they might create preconceptions which would not be easy to change afterward no matter how we tried. Hence, the training was originally meant not to be publicized, but it soon became an open matter, and everyone started to go door-knocking.

Generally speaking, knocking on doors is very easy. Who does not know how to do it? It seems that even a child can do it. On the other hand, some who saw this practice "blew cold wind," saying, "What is the difference between this door-knocking and the Mormons' door-knocking?" Apparently, the Mormons' success is founded on door-knocking. Where then is the differentiation? This is a particular point of concern—one kind of door-knocking is in fact vastly different from another.

In the past when a few localities in the United States began door-knocking, it was not very effective. However, some among them joined the training and returned to be "coaches" after the training, teaching others how to knock on doors. As a result, they have reaped the benefits. In one particular locality fifty saints went out and baptized more than forty people within three days, and some even set up home meetings. This opened the eyes of many to see that there is a difference between being trained and being untrained and that one kind of door-knocking is different from another. Thus, different localities in the United States hoped to come to be trained. Not only the elders wanted to come, but even those being trained to be elders, with others also who had a heart to pursue the Lord in the churches, all wanted to come. For this reason, we set up short-term training sessions, adopting an allocation system to assign fifty seat numbers for each locality. Each seat number was shared by one group of three persons. One training session lasted four months, which is one hundred twenty days in total. Thus, each of the three persons could participate for forty days. The first one came for the first forty days, occupying a certain seat; then the second one came, and after that the third. In this way, if there were ninety-five elders and fifty-five of those learning to be elders, all one hundred fifty could join the training. I believe that they were able to make an impact in different places after they returned from the training.

One elder who joined a two-week training session learned some secrets and practiced according to the new way when he returned. He testified that he had been in the church life for over twenty years, being an elder for fourteen or fifteen years, but had not brought one person to the Lord. At this time, however, he baptized seventeen persons within four months and another four persons in a following month, totaling twenty-one. All of these twenty-one persons were his fruit of only five months. There is no comparison between not bringing one person to the Lord in fourteen or fifteen years and baptizing twenty-one people in five months after practicing the new way. This showed us that the new way was absolutely effective, even lovely in the eyes of many people. Recently, of the number that came from the United States to be full-time trainees, less than sixty returned; the remaining ninety-two stayed to continue with the training. Leaving their hometown was not an easy thing, but it was wonderful that once they came, they did not want to leave. That is why we say that the training is lovely.

CONCERNING THE STATISTICS AND ESTIMATION TO EVANGELIZE THE WHOLE EARTH

Our research concludes that to succeed in the new way there are two principles: first, to produce one full-timer out of every twenty saints, and second, that one-fourth of the number who meet should set aside two to three hours to go door-knocking, four weeks a month, fifty-two weeks a year, continuously week by week. As long as we practice this principle, we will see the result. A church with a base number of one hundred people can produce five full-timers. If these five go door-knocking five days per week, two to three hours per day, they each will baptize at least one person a week. This should not be difficult; everyone should be able to do it. In this way, one person can gain one a week, which is approximately fifty a year. Thus, five persons can gain two hundred fifty in a year.

Besides the full-timers, among the basic number of one hundred there are another twenty-five "job-holding full-timers." They can go visiting once a week, two or three hours each time continually for four weeks in a month. (Among one hundred saints who meet, after deducting five full-timers and another twenty-five who go out once a week, there are still seventy saints on reserve. Therefore, in reality only thirty saints are mobilized.) According to our estimation, each of the twenty-five should be able to baptize one person in four weeks. Thus, in the fifty-two weeks of the year, three hundred people can be brought in, which, added to the two hundred fifty gained by the full-timers, increases the total to five hundred fifty. Adding this to the original base number of one hundred, the grand total is six hundred fifty people. To add five hundred fifty to one hundred is a five-and-a-half-fold increase.

Calculating further from the first and second years, the total by the third year will be over sixteen thousand people. From one hundred as the original base, the number will exceed sixteen thousand after working for three years. Using a more conservative calculation, we simply may say that ten thousand can be gained in three years from a base of one hundred people, which is a hundredfold increase. One hundred can become ten thousand in the first three years, from 1987 to 1989. Then using ten thousand as the base, another hundredfold increase in the three years from 1990 to 1992 will produce one million. Therefore, if beginning from 1987 we all truly practice according to this new way, one hundred will become one million in six years.

Using again one million as the base and another hundredfold increase in the three years from 1993 to 1995, the total number will be one hundred million. Then after another hundredfold increase from 1996 to 1998, the total will be ten billion, which is twice the present world population of five billion, one-fifth of which is in China. Thus, twelve years takes us through four rounds of multiplication: the first turning one hundred into ten thousand, the second turning ten thousand into one million, the third turning one million into one hundred million, and the fourth turning one hundred million into ten billion. In this way, we can evangelize twice the number of people on the earth. As such, this way is too good; in only twelve years we will be able to see the result of evangelizing the entire earth.

Perhaps some will ask if this is too quick, too ideal, and not practical. For their sake, we can calculate in another way. If there are one hundred people meeting in a church, and these one hundred all go out to knock on doors every week, each person should be able to gain one person to be baptized every two months. By the third year, there will be close to five thousand persons, which is a fiftyfold increase. After several more rounds there will be five billion, the total world population. This is very wonderful indeed!

CONCERNING THE STATISTICS AND ESTIMATION TO EVANGELIZE TAIWAN

The current total population of Taiwan is nineteen million. At present there are six hundred full-timers here. If they go out to knock on doors every week this year, each one will baptize fifty-two people. Even if they cannot do this, they will baptize at least forty. In this way, twenty-four thousand people will be saved.

Previously, there were approximately ten thousand saints meeting regularly in the whole of Taiwan, more than 3,500 of whom are in Taipei. Of the over eight thousand who were baptized last year, about one out of four are stable in the church life. Adding these two thousand stable ones to the original ten thousand, we have a base number of twelve thousand. For one-fourth of these to go out to knock on doors weekly means that three thousand are going. If each of these gains one person every two months, that is, six a year, eighteen thousand people will be saved. Adding these to the original twelve thousand saints and the twenty-four thousand gained by the full-timers, there will be a total of fifty-four thousand saints in all of Taiwan by the end of this year. This is a law that we discovered from the training, a figure that we calculated scientifically; every saint should see this.

After this, in 1988 there will be at least one thousand full-timers. If each gains forty persons, there will be forty thousand people. If one-fourth of the fifty-four thousand calculated above each gains six in a year, there will be eighty-one thousand. Adding this number to the original fifty-four thousand and the forty thousand gained by the full-timers, the total then will be 175,000. With this kind of accumulation through 1989, the result will be 477,500, which we may round up to 480,000. This is a fortyfold increase from the original base number of twelve thousand. Another fortyfold increase in the next round will result in 19,200,000. Therefore, within six years, by 1992, every one of the nineteen million people in Taiwan will have been sought out by us, unless, of course, someone is a son of perdition. By that time Taiwan will be evangelized; the gospel will have saturated Taiwan.

THE KEY TO SUCCESS IN THE NEW WAY

Producing Full-timers to Practice Door-knocking in a Serious Way

For this, we must practically study our estimates in order to find the reliable, crucial points for our practice. According to our experience, we must practice the following points in order to have each full-timer baptize forty persons in a year. First, the full-timers themselves must be produced. This is not a problem in Taiwan, because there are already one thousand who have registered for the training. There will definitely be six hundred full-timers starting next month. Although it sounds very easy to have one thousand people each baptizing forty in a year, it will require their labor from house to house. If these one thousand are merely dreaming day after day, thinking that our estimate is unreal and because of this being at ease, then they may not be able to baptize even twenty persons.

It is practical to expect that the one-fourth in the church who have a heart to go door-knocking once a week can gain six persons in a year. However, we fear that they may "fish only for three days and dry their nets for two days," eventually becoming unfruitful. To gain people properly requires us to be in one accord and to work seriously. To be sure, working seriously will produce results. This is the first key to success in the new way.

Setting Up Home Meetings as a Covering and Protection to the New Ones

We also need to lead the home meetings in a good way. This is more difficult than the first point, but if the home meetings are unsuccessful, the new way cannot proceed. The one-fourth in the church who have the heart will continue to increase in number; therefore, they will need much perfecting. In John 15:16 the Lord Jesus first said, "You should go forth and bear fruit"; after this He said, "That your fruit should remain." Whether or not the fruit remains is not on the Lord's side but on ours. If we work well, this will cause our fruit to remain. The Lord also reveals to us that it is the home meetings that cause our fruit to remain (see footnote 3 of verse 16 in the Recovery Version).

Previously, out of one hundred people whom we baptized, perhaps not even five would remain. This can be compared to a woman who, having given birth to some children, feels that she has finished her duty and does not raise them up. Because of this, one hundred may be delivered, but only five survive; the remaining ninety-five die prematurely. This is because there is no nourishing and supporting through the home meetings. At this time, though, we have the home meetings, which are a safeguard for the newly baptized ones. Once a person is baptized, we should immediately arrange a home meeting for him. As soon as a home meeting is started, this newly baptized one will have a safeguard, covering, and protection. The modern medical technology in America is very advanced. A baby born prematurely can still grow properly after he is delivered. This is because as soon as the baby is born, he is put into an incubator. The incubator becomes his way to survive. Our home meetings are the "incubators" for the new ones.

After bringing a person to be saved, we must nourish and teach him. When a certain young man was born prematurely, he was small and wrinkled. Those who saw him lying in the incubator had to exercise their faith because they did not know how he could grow up. Today, however, he has become tall and strong and is a soccer player in school. This was possible only because he was properly taken care of after he was born. This is what we are saying about our home meetings. We cannot merely baptize people. Of course, we long for more births, yet if we do not nourish and teach those who are baptized, they will die prematurely. The home meetings provide the nourishing and teaching for people after they are saved and baptized. In the spiritual sense, to teach is to nourish. The more we teach people the truth, the more the riches contained in the truth will supply and nourish them. Hence, the home meeting is the second key to success in the new way.

A FEW GUIDELINES
CONCERNING THE HOME MEETINGS

We can summarize the need in the home meetings in four crucial points, which we need to pay close attention to.

Seeing That the Old Way
Kills the Function of the Believers

First, never bring the old practice into the home meetings; this will kill the function of the believers. When we go to the homes of the newly baptized ones to lead the home meetings, whether in singing, praying, reading the Bible, or fellowshipping, we cannot use the old method. We hope all of our concepts will be changed regarding this point. What is the old way? It is the way in which everything in a meeting is cared for by those who lead the meeting. The selection of hymns, the singing, the praying, the reading of the Bible, the giving of messages, and even the concluding of the meeting are all carried out by those who lead the meeting. Consequently, when a newly baptized person comes to the meeting, he dares not do anything except remain in his seat, because those who lead the meeting do everything. This is the old way, the old method, which nullifies the function of the believers.

It is easy for the old way to produce a clergy. In addition, organization emerges unconsciously from the old way, and once there is organization, there is control. In such a condition, there is no way for the newly baptized ones to function. Originally, a newly saved one may have been very active, but once he comes to the meetings, he can no longer be active, because the practice of the old way immobilizes, even kills, him. Gradually, he loses his spiritual sensation, coming merely to believe that a Christian should love the Lord, pursue Him, and come to the meetings regularly. Eventually, even though he comes to the meetings, he does not have any feeling, like a person who has been drugged. Although he is alive and still breathing, he has no spiritual consciousness.

Seeing That the Old Way
Deprives the Believers of their Organic Function

Second, we need to see that the old way deprives the believers of their organic function. We have to realize that if we remain in this old way of meeting, after half a year we will be "anesthetized" and unable to wake up. As we said earlier, a brother among us admitted to having been an elder for over ten years yet not having brought one person to the Lord nor having had any realization or feeling that this was a very serious matter. In the Gospel of John, the Lord said that He takes away every branch that does not bear fruit (15:2). This is a terrible thing. What does it mean to take away a branch? To take away a branch cannot be a good thing. For a branch in the vine to be taken away means that it has nothing to do with any of the riches of the vine. This is not a question of whether or not you will perish; it simply means that you will certainly not be able to enjoy the Lord's riches.

Logically speaking, the enjoyment of the Lord should issue in a rich fruit-bearing. How can a brother be an elder for a long time, not bring one person to the Lord, and still not have any sensation about it? This is to be drugged, even to be in a "coma," alive and breathing but with no feeling at all. This is a grave matter. The old kind of meetings kill and drug the members of the Body of Christ. Therefore, we can no longer take the old way of practice in the meetings. Rather, we must absolutely abandon it.

Helping the New Ones
to Establish Proper Home Meetings

Third, we must help the new ones to establish proper

home meetings. This includes three main items: how to teach people the truth, how to nourish people for growth in life, and how to lead people to know the church. To lead the home meetings properly is the crucial key to the new practice in the new way. At present, there is no problem in bringing in new ones; many babies are being born. Rather, the question is how to nurture the babies after they are born. To begin with, the old method cannot be brought into the new meetings. According to this principle, we have to study how to call the hymns, read the Bible, and pray in the home meetings in order to purge the old practice of having everything taken care of by a few. We should not tolerate that a newly baptized person in the meeting is influenced by those who lead the meeting to the point that he loses the exercise of his normal function.

In addition, we have to make appointments for home meetings after baptizing people. The new ones may not know how to meet the first time we go, so we have to teach them how to have a home meeting. We must tell them that this meeting is a meeting for their family and that we are there only to help. We also have to tell them that Christian meetings are nothing apart from singing hymns, reading the Lord's Word, testifying, sharing, and preaching the gospel when gospel friends come. We should let them know that a meeting is simply a matter of these things, which should not be carried out by the so-called responsible ones. Almost everyone in a home meeting is a newly saved one. In this sense, there are no elders, deacons, or even any leading ones. Everyone has to function and take care of his own meeting. Initially, when we go to help the new ones in a home meeting, we will at most fellowship with them and demonstrate to them in the meeting how to pray, sing the hymns, and read the Scriptures, but we must allow them to do these on their own as much as possible.

Not Replacing the Organic Function
of the New Ones

Fourth, do not replace the organic function of the new ones as members. When we begin a home meeting, there is no need of a formal opening. When the parents begin to clean and arrange chairs after dinner, the children know that it is time to meet, so they joyfully sing, "You need Jesus, you need Jesus." Once the children start singing, the meeting has already begun. When others arrive and hear the children singing, they will spontaneously join them, and the father and mother will also follow in the singing. It is the same with praying. Perhaps when dinner and cleaning are almost finished, the father will begin to pray, "O Lord, we thank You that we all are saved, and today we can come together to enjoy You. We thank You also for sending a brother to help us." At this point, the meeting has begun. Instead, perhaps, no one sings or prays after the meal, but someone reads Genesis 1:1: "In the beginning God created the heavens and the earth." This also begins the meeting. There is no need for someone else to lead a home meeting; it is those in the home who lead the meeting themselves. This is the way to call hymns, pray, and read the Bible in the new practice.

It is the same with testifying. Perhaps after the meal the mother says to the children, "Children, see how great the Lord's grace is! We used to worship idols in darkness." The mother is actually testifying when she speaks in this way, thus beginning the home meeting. It is not necessary to wait until 7:00 to begin, and there is no need to rely on someone else. Those in the family can start the meeting. The father may say, "Children, select a hymn," or the children may not wait for the father but will start singing, "Since Jesus came into my heart." We have to teach all the new ones in this way when they begin to meet after being saved, just as a mother helps her child to eat after giving birth to him. All mothers realize that they have to help children to eat and not eat for them.

Moreover, once the new ones have established a home meeting, we have to help them to appreciate the hymns. Each one should have a hymnal. They need to learn how to sing the hymns, but not only in the meetings. Even at home a mother can learn to sing by playing a cassette tape while she washes dishes. We all know that young children learn how to talk and sing by listening. People who are unable to hear are also unable to sing or talk. If circumstances allow, we need to help the new ones to listen more to song tapes at home. Then it will be easy for them to sing. Initially, they can sing short songs, such as "You Need Jesus" and "Since Jesus Came into My Heart." We should also urge them to own a Bible in order to read the Lord's Word daily.

How to teach people the truth, how to nourish them, how to help them grow in life, and how to help them know the church in order to enter into the church life are all items for our study. Do not hastily bring the new ones to the church meetings after they are baptized. The most precious of the various church meetings is the Lord's table meeting. Therefore, we have to lead them to meet to break bread, but we must continue to study how to bring them to the other meetings.

A QUESTION AND ANSWER

Question: When we go to the home meetings, we are all prepared, having prayed and come into the meeting in the spirit. However, when we stop speaking in the meeting, the new ones also stop. Even though we truly do not want to speak too much, we still have to speak. What shall we do?

Answer: We have to do our best not to replace the function of the new ones. Our speaking too much will not perfect people. After making an appointment with the new ones for their first home meeting, we need to give them an opening word to help them understand that this meeting is their meeting and that the meetings of Christians are nothing more than praying, reading the Bible, singing, testifying, and exhorting one another. We have to lay this foundation the first time we go and show them how to conduct the meetings, encouraging them to start the meeting themselves and not to wait for each other. Each one may have a hymn, a word from the Lord, or a testimony. All these are proper practices for the meetings.

What we have fellowshipped here is the new way of meeting without any formality. We need to make this way clear to people the first time we go to their home to meet. We should not completely carry out the meeting, replacing their function to lead the singing and praying. To do so is to go back to the old way. When a mother teaches her child to speak, she knows that he should speak correctly from the beginning. If a child habitually mispronounces a word, it will be difficult to correct him later. We must pay close attention to all of the above points.

(A message given on January 28, 1987 in Taipei, Taiwan)

Chapter Two

THE FUTURE PROSPECT OF
THE SUCCESS OF THE NEW WAY

THE STUDY FOR THE FURTHERANCE OF THE NEW WAY

It is not easy for anyone to leave their old ways and habits. Even without purposely expressing them, a person's old habits and ways will come out. For a person to build up a new way is not an easy matter. Door-knocking and home meetings are an example of this; no matter how we carry them out, our doing may still be in the old way because we have been in the old way for too long.

In principle, to meet in homes is more difficult than door-knocking. We cannot find precisely from the Bible how the Lord wants us to meet. One thing is certain, though: The Bible clearly says, "According to the spirit" (Rom. 8:5). "According to the spirit" is easy to say, but the phrase *according to* still indicates a way; this requires us to spend more time to study. We must also be ready to encounter setbacks, disappointments, distractions, and pressures during our process of studying how to have home meetings. We may use the example of children learning to play the piano. Children are very wild at first, playing in the way they want to. Therefore, the teacher must apply strict control and limit the students, teaching them to play with only two or three fingers at a time and to practice at least one hour every day, applying a certain amount of pressure on them. This "pressure" produces an ability in them. Olives do not give oil without pressure; once pressure is applied, the oil comes out. Therefore, do not be disappointed. The secret of door-knocking is to be excited, but the secret of meeting in homes is to not be disappointed.

THE RE-ESTIMATION
OF THE GOSPELIZATION OF TAIWAN

In order for anything to have results, it is necessary to make estimates and keep statistics. Estimating and keeping statistics are the guidelines of a business. Without estimating there is no preparation. The more estimates we make and the more detailed they are, the more adequate our preparation will be and the more reliable our work will turn out.

For this reason, we need to redo our estimates. First, we will assume that the number of those meeting in the churches in Taipei and in the whole of Taiwan is ten thousand. Of course, the number on our lists is larger than this by several-fold, especially if we include the seven to eight thousand who were baptized through door-knocking last year. Nevertheless, in 1987 we set the base number simply as ten thousand.

In principle, every church should produce one full-timer for every twenty saints meeting regularly, which is five percent of the total number. If we take ten thousand as the base number, five hundred full-timers should be produced. Every full-timer who goes out door-knocking every day for two to three hours is bound to see one person saved and baptized in less than a week. This is what we have already experienced. However, according to our actual church life it is not possible to go door-knocking every week for fifty-two weeks of the year. Sometimes there are trainings and certain church activities, and sometimes a person may become sick and need a few days to rest. Therefore, we can set aside four weeks for time off and still use forty-eight weeks for work. Five working days every week for forty-eight weeks is two hundred forty days. If someone goes door-knocking two to three hours every day, and in six days he gains one person, then in one year he can gain forty people. Forty times five hundred full-timers is twenty thousand. Even this number is very conservative, but the smaller the number we use, the more accurate and realistic it can be. If our standard is too high, I am afraid we may not be able to attain to it.

In regard to how many new ones will remain, we need to apply a significant discount. We know that there are always losses in a factory. We may use pottery as an example. Out of one hundred pots in a batch there may be ten that do not pass quality control inspections due to defects or breakage. These must be discarded, which is a loss of ten percent. Then during distribution there is another quality control check to examine the products. If the decorative design on a pot has a small defect which is detected by a close inspection, it will not be distributed to the regular market but will be sold elsewhere at a reduced price. It is the same with the manufacture of garments and articles of wood. Every industry encounters the problem of loss in the production process. Eventually, perhaps only sixty to seventy percent of the products are up to the proper standard. It is the same with the printing of books. Sometimes there are books with missing or upside down pages; these must be thrown away. In farming, the planting of vegetables and orchards have the same problem. Farmers must account for losses due to pests, floods, a scorching sun, and substandard harvests. After accounting for all the losses, what remains may not be very much.

Based on this principle, in fellowship we have estimated that only thirty-five percent of the seven thousand five hundred people we gained last year have remained. Therefore, if we gain twenty thousand people from door-knocking, the actual number of those who remain will be seven thousand.

Next we must consider the saints meeting regularly in the church who have the heart to go door-knocking. According to our calculation, and using ten thousand as the base number, twenty-five percent, or one-quarter, of the saints go door-knocking once a week. One-quarter of ten thousand people is two thousand five hundred. Counting forty-eight weeks as one year, if each gains one person every six weeks, he will gain eight people per year. Eight times two thousand five hundred saints is another gain of twenty thousand people.

Thus, we have a conclusion. The result of one full-timer's work equals that of five saints who go out door-knocking once a week. The number of people gained by these two categories of saints is the same. Five percent who go out daily gain twenty thousand, and twenty-five percent who go out once a week also gain twenty thousand. Please remember, though, that there is the discount of sixty-five percent. The remaining number of each category is seven thousand, so the two categories added together make fourteen thousand. Using ten thousand as the base number, after one year of work there is the gain of fourteen thousand, which is then added to the original ten thousand. Therefore, by the end of 1987 there should be at least twenty-four thousand people, which is an increase of two hundred forty percent.

In 1988 the base number becomes twenty-four thousand, which multiplied by 2.4 becomes 57,600 by the end of the year. Using the latter figure as the new base number and multiplying again by 2.4, the result at the end of 1989 is 138,240 people. Therefore, using ten thousand as the original number, after laboring for one round of three years, the total is an increase of 13.8 times.

From 1990 to 1992 is a second round of three years. Using 138,240 as the base number and multiplying by 13.8, the result is just over 1,907,000. Using this as the base of the third and last round, from 1993 to 1995, the result after multiplying by 13.8 is over 26,300,000. By this time the total number has surpassed the population of Taiwan. In other words, Taiwan will be "gospelized."

The population of Taiwan at present is more than nineteen million. In three rounds of three years each, twenty-six million people can be saved. Reaching this number in only nine years seems very astonishing. We are using only ten thousand as the base number, without including others. Furthermore, one full-timer out of every twenty people and one out of four who goes door-knocking once a week is not a high percentage. Out of the ten thousand saints there are five hundred full-timers and two thousand five hundred weekly door-knockers. This leaves seven thousand others who pray, give, and support those who go out. Three thousand go out to fight, and seven thousand remain stationed. The three thousand who go out to fight are like the three hundred warriors of Gideon (Judg. 7:5-7). These need the prayers of the seven thousand behind them as well as their material supply.

These statistics and estimates are not unrealistic. Out of ten thousand, if three thousand go to the front line and seven thousand remain as support, those who go out can go forward boldly without anxiety. The five hundred full-timers who go out forty-eight weeks, two hundred forty days, door-knocking every day for two to three hours, should be able to gain one person in six days. The two thousand five hundred who go out once weekly also gain one person every six days in which they labor. The statistics for the rate of gaining people in each of the two categories is the same, each group gaining twenty thousand. Assuming that thirty-five percent of these remain, out of twenty thousand we still have seven thousand for each category, fourteen thousand in all. Adding these to the original ten thousand, the total is twenty-four thousand people. Working according to this rate, which is an increase of two hundred forty percent, one hundred becomes two hundred forty, one thousand becomes two thousand four hundred, and ten thousand becomes twenty-four thousand. This calculation of the original base number, the number of full-timers, the number who go out once a week, and the discount due to loss is a very conservative expectation. Even still, after working for nine years, ten thousand can become twenty-six million. This number is astonishing!

EXAMPLES OF STRIVING FOR PREACHING THE GOSPEL THROUGH DOOR-KNOCKING

If we agree with this way and do not oppose it, then the full-timers should go door-knocking two to three hours every day. In two and a half hours someone can knock on the doors of fifteen homes, and in six days he can knock on ninety homes. Among these ninety homes there should be at least one "son of peace" (Luke 10:5-6). If someone goes out the first week and there is no son of peace, and on the second, third, and even sixth week there still is none, he may go to the Lord desperately and say, "Lord, I give up. Without finding a son of peace there is no meaning to my living. In these six weeks I have not been able to find even one. Lord, have You taken away all the sons of peace, just like You chased away all the fish from Peter for the whole night in John 21? What can I do now?" I believe if someone endeavors in this way and goes out again the seventh week, there will be at least two sons of peace.

In a certain church in the United States, a brother gave the following testimony. One Saturday evening he went out door-knocking with some brothers and sisters. Everyone was doing their best. They went to about twenty homes, but they could not find even one son of peace. Eventually everyone wanted to go home. He said, "All right, you can go home, but I will continue. I must gain one person and baptize him. Otherwise, I will not eat or sleep." Thank the Lord, at the twenty-first door he knocked on, he gained a son of peace. If we are willing to go door-knocking and are willing to have a serious transaction with the Lord, I believe that the Lord will respond to us.

A brother in North Carolina gave this testimony. He went with some who were knocking on doors for three days, yet he could not gain even one. He was upset to the uttermost and even felt shameful. Then he repented greatly before the Lord, cried, emptied himself, and asked for the filling of the Holy Spirit. The following day, the fourth day of door-knocking, he went again. That day he gained three people. This way is truly workable, and this method is definitely successful. We need only nine years, with ten thousand as our base number and three thousand to go out. Then we can reach twenty-six million people. Is this not extremely workable?

SHARING THE REWARD
BY PRAYING AND GIVING FOR DOOR-KNOCKING

Even though approximately seventy percent of the saints do not go out, they still can pray, give, and supply. Of those Israelites who followed Gideon, eventually only ten thousand remained (Judg. 7:1-3). However, God said to Gideon, "The people are still too many" (v. 4). God wanted Gideon to choose three hundred among them. It is the same principle here. Of the ten thousand enlisted soldiers, we choose three thousand to fight. Of course, when the time for reward comes, they will get the prize first; nevertheless, the seven thousand will be the next to get the prize.

The estimation we have made for the rate of people being saved cannot be any lower. I do not know how many times we need to knock on the doors of the people on the whole of

Taiwan before they all will be saved. In Luke 10 when the Lord Jesus was sending out the seventy disciples, He said, "I send you as lambs in the midst of wolves" (v. 3). Even though they were in the midst of wolves, there were sons of peace among the wolves. Today who among society is a son of peace? Who will receive the gospel willingly? When we go out door-knocking, we will find out who the sons of peace are. When someone opens the door, we will know if he is a son of peace. Someone may not be a son of peace today, but he will be one tomorrow. In Taipei, we have gone door-knocking at two hundred thousand homes, which is over one-third of whole of the island. In the future we must knock on their doors again, until 1995 when all the sons of peace are found and become Christians. What a glorious result this will be!

SOME BASIC PRINCIPLES OF THE HOME MEETINGS

Once a person is saved, we need to help him to have a home meeting. The principles of attending a home meeting are first that we must make a resolution, and second that we must know that our going to the home meetings is not to lead the new ones but to teach them. We go there as "coaches" to open up their hearts and teach them the basic functions of a meeting, just as a basketball coach first teaches his team the basic actions of the game. The basic actions of a home meeting include praying, singing hymns, reading the Bible, expounding the Word, giving testimonies, and encouraging one another. There are at least six or seven basic actions that the new ones need to become familiar with.

In the first few meetings you can use some of the subjects from *Life Lessons* such as prayer and reading the Bible. Then you can help them exercise to pray and read the Bible. On the third week you can teach them to sing hymns. You can tell them that anyone can sing. If they want to learn to sing more, they can obtain a set of tapes from *One Hundred Selected Hymns* and listen to them at home. Perhaps some hymns are difficult to understand, but the more someone listens to them, the more he becomes familiar with the tune and the music. You must teach the new ones item by item.

When we go to their home meetings and teach them these six or seven basic actions, we can tell them that this meeting is like a ball game, and we are simply the coaches who coach them how to play. Actually, we ourselves do not play, but they play. Then when they need some improvement, we will spontaneously correct them. Once they have this basic concept, they will exercise to function. In addition, we must also meet some incidental needs, showing them, for example, how we differ from Christianity and why our meetings are different from those in Christianity. We can also show them the example of baptism in Acts 8; once the eunuch was saved and wanted to be baptized, Philip baptized him in the water by the roadside (vv. 35-39). There is also the account of the jailer in Philippi whom Paul baptized in the jailer's own house (16:30-33). In the Bible we do not find a baptistery. We must let them know this point, so that by giving them some principles, if they have heard something wrong or confusing, we can help them to walk according to the truth. This is the way to take care of their incidental needs.

QUESTIONS AND ANSWERS

Question: The full-timers are supposed to gain one person every six days. If three of them go together, does it mean that they should gain three people a week in order to fulfill this count?

Answer: If three go out together and gain one person every two days, in six days they will gain three people. On the average each gains one person.

Question: According to statistics there is no problem with our estimates. However, normally the full-timers have much work and service, and they also have to go to many home meetings. Because of this we do not have the confidence we can attain to this goal.

Answer: We must consider and discuss the assignment of persons in taking care of the home meetings. As an example, if there are twenty-five hundred people who go out once a week, once they bear fruit and home meetings are set up, they must add another time to go out every week. This is not an assignment given to them by others. Rather, once they bear a child, they will spontaneously love him. Even without others urging them, they will go to take care of their child. In the future it is possible to have the one in four who goes door-knocking to go out at least twice a week, one time for door-knocking and another for caring for a home meeting.

There are twelve thousand new ones among us. Since on the average there are at least two new ones in each home, there are about six thousand homes. Besides the manpower of the two thousand five hundred saints, the five hundred full-timers can also help in taking care of these homes. They will go out five days a week and attend home meetings at least three evenings, and if necessary, five evenings. Five hundred full-timers going out for five days is the equivalent of two thousand five hundred more persons to bear this burden. Added to the first two thousand five hundred saints, this will equal the manpower of five thousand people to take care of six thousand homes per week. This should be sufficient to meet the need.

THE FUTURE PROSPECT OF THE SUCCESS OF THE NEW WAY

We have the faith that the new way can bring the gospel to the whole inhabited earth. If the Lord has mercy on us so that we work out our estimate, then the people on the whole of Taiwan will be saved. This matter is so great that it shakes the universe. Consider this: Of twenty million Christians, every twenty will produce one full-timer, which makes one million full-timers. These one million should all be university graduates who are fluent in international languages, spreading out to the whole world. Then they will be able to conquer the whole world with the gospel. Not only so, each of the twenty million should offer material support out of their monthly income. If each one has a monthly income of three hundred dollars, he can give thirty dollars per month. Twenty million times thirty dollars is six hundred million dollars. This is very remarkable. At that time, much manpower and material riches will be given for the gospel, and the gospel will be spread throughout the whole world.

We truly look to the Lord to accomplish this. We believe

that He is sovereign over all things and will certainly fulfill this matter. If He truly accomplishes this, then first of all the whole population of the island of the Republic of China will become Christians. This will shock the entire world. Second, with one million full-timers sent out, the gospel will be preached to the whole world. Third, the offering of millions of dollars to follow the full-timers will truly be a great feat. We all know that in the past ten or more years, the Lord has richly released the truths among us. When we go out, we do not go empty-handed, but we bring the truths to the whole world. This is the spreading of the gospel of the kingdom to the whole inhabited earth (Matt. 24:14). Therefore, we have the assurance that this is a practical way that will take us toward fulfilling our estimate.

(A message given on January 29, 1987 in Taipei, Taiwan)

CHAPTER THREE

BEING WITH THE LORD, LIVING WITH THE LORD, AND BEARING FRUIT WITH THE LORD

THE SECRET OF FRUIT-BEARING

The secret of fruit-bearing lies in prayer, confessing of sins, and being filled with the Holy Spirit. John 15:16 says, "You did not choose Me, but I chose you, and I set you that you should go forth and bear fruit and that your fruit should remain, that whatever you ask the Father in My name, He may give you." Many people do not understand why, after the Lord says that we should bear fruit and that our fruit should remain, He immediately says that whatever we ask the Father in His name, the Father may give us. Why does the Lord connect the answering of prayer to fruit-bearing and having remaining fruit?

Then verse 17 says, "These things I command you that you may love one another." It is difficult to discover the relationship between these few things—bearing fruit and having remaining fruit, having our prayers answered, and loving one another—and it is not easy to apprehend according to our logic. The fact is that to love one another is to be in one accord. Both bearing fruit and having our prayer answered depend on our being in one accord. This is the secret that relates to fruit-bearing, answered prayer, and loving one another.

BEARING REMAINING FRUIT DEPENDING ON THE HOME MEETINGS

Throughout this year more than thirteen thousand people have been baptized in Taipei. If we do not conduct our home meetings well, and if there is not enough support, there will certainly be some new ones who will slip away. John 15:16 says, "That your fruit should remain." The Lord does not want us only to bear fruit; He also desires that our fruit would remain. Knocking on doors and bringing people to salvation is to bear fruit; conducting home meetings is to have the fruit remain. When we visit people by knocking on their doors, bringing them to salvation and baptizing them, we are begetting them. Then home meetings are the nourishing after people have been begotten. All mothers know that a child must be nursed after he is born. If the child is not nursed after he is born, he will surely die.

If we gain thirteen thousand new ones, but eventually we lose twelve thousand, with very few who remain, the saints will be discouraged. Therefore, we have to endeavor to raise up these new believers one by one. This depends altogether on the home meetings. How the home meetings are conducted is one of the ultimate secrets to the success of the new way. We knock on doors, bring people to salvation, and baptize them, yet doing all this is not the conclusion. As we all know, even the Mormons and Jehovah's Witnesses rise up to knock on doors. However, these are two great heresies, which have differing and wrong opinions concerning the person of the Lord Jesus. They do not confess that the Lord Jesus is God, yet their door-knocking has been very effective. Therefore, knocking on doors to bring people to salvation is not the conclusion. We still need to ensure that the fruit we bear remains.

This is a test with two aspects. On one hand, we bring many people to salvation, but on the other hand, we must face the issue of whether or not these people will remain. We can say that we have won the battle of bringing people to salvation. However, this victory still needs a confirmation, a conclusion. This confirmation, conclusion, depends on the home meetings, on whether or not the fruit gained from door-knocking is living and remaining.

OUR EMPHASIS IN THE PAST
BEING CHRIST, THE SPIRIT, LIFE, AND THE CHURCH

We previously did not have much light concerning the practice of the new way. In the past we emphasized the four lines of Christ, the Spirit, life, and the church. We have spoken of Christ being the Triune God, who became a man, passed through human living, went to the cross, entered into death, and resurrected from death to become the life-giving Spirit. As such a One He has entered into us and dwells in our spirit to be our life and element, not only to regenerate us but even the more to transform us. Thereafter, He constitutes us to be the church, which is His Body as His fullness. In addition, the churches which appear in every locality are His living testimony. This is the line we have paid attention to in the past.

This Christ is the Spirit. If He were God and Christ but not the Spirit, He could have nothing to do with us. On the one hand, He has a relationship with us because He is the Creator and we are the creation; He is God and we are men. On the other hand, He would not have an organic relationship, an organic union, with us. He could not enter into us, and neither could we enter into Him. He could contact us, but He could not join Himself to us. According to His heart's desire, He wants not only to be joined to us but also to mingle with us. He wants to become us and that we would become Him. This would be impossible without the organic union. If Christ were not the Spirit, He would have no way to have an organic union with us, to be our life, and to abide in us. Therefore, Christ must be the Spirit. In John 15 the Lord says, "I am the vine; you are the branches. He who abides in Me and I in him" (v. 5). This is the organic union. Such a union is not like the binding together of two pieces of dead wood or the welding of two pieces of iron or steel. Rather, it is a living tree having living branches in a union of life. This is altogether a matter of life. If God and Christ were not the Spirit, how could He have such a life union with us?

For sixty years the light that God has continually granted us has been first concerning Christ and second concerning the Spirit. When Brother Watchman Nee was with us, he fellowshipped very clearly concerning the first aspect. He also paid attention to the second aspect, but he did not have the time to fellowship clearly about it. In 1952 Brother Nee was put into jail. Since then I have had within me a heavy burden that I must speak clearly concerning Christ being the Spirit.

The first message that I spoke concerning Christ being the Spirit was released in Manila. Then when I was in Taiwan, I spoke further concerning this. By the time I came to the United States, the burden within me had become even heavier. At that time there was a dear co-worker who warned me, saying, "The Bible truly speaks about the Spirit of Christ, telling us that Christ is the Spirit. However, you cannot speak this in America because Christianity here will not receive it." He had a good intention, but his good intention was with disagreement. We may have much doctrine and knowledge of the Bible, but if we do not know that Christ is the Spirit, those doctrines are not related to us in a real way, and we have no taste for them. It is only when Christ as the Spirit enters into us that all the spiritual realities are brought to us. The One who was crucified, passed through death, resurrected, and entered into us has become the Spirit, the reality. The One on the cross is Christ, but the One who enters into us is the Spirit. I told that co-worker that speaking on Christ being the Spirit was my burden; if I did not speak this, I would have nothing to say. Therefore, I have to speak this.

In 1962 at the beginning of our work in America, I first released *The All-inclusive Christ,* and after that I fellowshipped on Christ being the Spirit. There are two verses related to Christ being the Spirit. The first is 1 Corinthians 15:45b, which says, "The last Adam became a life-giving Spirit." However, many in Christianity do not understand this. They say, "This simply means that Christ has a Spirit, just as you and I have a spirit." However, this portion of the Bible does not say that the last Adam, Christ in the flesh, has a Spirit. Rather, it says that the last Adam has become a life-giving Spirit. There is a distinct adjective here: Christ has become a *life-giving* Spirit. If this life-giving Spirit is not the Holy Spirit, how can He give life? If He is not the Holy Spirit, then are there two life-giving Spirits in this universe? The second verse which tells us that Christ is the Spirit is 2 Corinthians 3:17; it says, "The Lord is the Spirit." Nothing can be clearer than this.

In the summer of 1969 in the conference in Erie, Pennsylvania, we released further messages on the seven Spirits. Many brothers in the United States can testify that the period of time after this may be considered the time when the churches in the United States were very living and high. Everyone enjoyed the burning of the seven Spirits.

Although for sixty years we have been holding to these four lines—Christ, the Spirit, life, and the church—we have to admit that on certain practical points we have had some problems, mainly concerning the preaching of the gospel. The majority of us have inherited the practice of Christianity, which is to give messages in a big congregation and invite people to come and listen. Throughout these decades, it is hard to say how many love feasts we have held and how many messages we have given. However, the result is that the number of people has not increased much. This is the situation in Taiwan and also in the United States.

THE LINE OF GOSPEL PREACHING IN THE BIBLE BEING RELATED TO THE HOMES

Our truth has been rich and high, and the light has been clear and bright in a way that is beyond comparison. However, before October 1984 our numbers were not increasing, and our fruit was not remaining. At that time, when we finished the life-study of the New Testament, we decided to go to Taiwan to research the reasons for this. As a result of this research, we have seen the line of gospel preaching in the Bible.

Most Christians feel that to speak about preaching the gospel is a common thing. Who does not know about preaching the gospel? Apparently, as long as someone knows how to speak, he knows how to preach the gospel. However, we all can testify that it is not effective to depend on only one person to preach. With only one person speaking and all the others listening again and again, there is not much remaining fruit. At this time the Lord is opening our eyes to show us a line that we have neglected, which is to "go" (Matt. 28:19) and to meet "from house to house" (Acts 2:46; 5:42).

In the past we had the rich truth, the high gospel, but the result of our going out to gain people was not satisfactory. This was because we did not go in the right way, and we did not pay attention to meeting in the homes. Therefore, there

was not much result. In the Bible we see the importance of
the homes. In the Old Testament there were the houses of
Israel in which the Passover was held, the house of Joshua,
the whole house of Rahab the harlot, the house of Jacob, and
the house of David (Exo. 12:3-4; Josh. 24:15; 6:17; Exo. 19:3;
Psa. 114:1; Zech. 12:7-8, 10; 13:1). In the New Testament
there is the house of Zaccheus, the house of Simon the Phari-
see, the house of Stephanas, the house of Lydia, and the house
of Mary, the mother of John Mark (Luke 19:5, 9; 7:36; 1 Cor.
1:16; 16:15; Acts 16:40; 12:12). Because of this, we know that
we must go to people's houses.

The first one in the universe who came to man was God
Himself. Although God created man, this man fell. The first
couple, Adam and Eve, fell together. They were so frightened
that they hid among the trees and made aprons out of fig
leaves, avoiding the face of God. God came to the garden of
Eden, walked in the garden, and cried to Adam, "Where are
you?" (Gen. 3:9). In other words, God said to Adam, "Do not
avoid Me. I have come to save you." This is the same as the
Lord's words in the New Testament: "For the Son of Man has
come to seek and to save that which is lost" (Luke 19:10). God
was the first one to visit man and seek man. Not only did
God Himself come, but He came with the gospel, telling Adam
and Eve that the seed of the woman would bruise the head
of the serpent (Gen. 3:15). God has come and brought to us
the true gospel.

THE SON OF MAN HAVING COME
TO SEEK AND TO SAVE THAT WHICH IS LOST

Four thousand years after Adam, God Himself came to be
a man. The infinite God became a finite man. Philippians 2:6
says that He existed "in the form of God." This phrase denotes
Christ's existence from the beginning. He existed in the form
of God from the beginning, but He laid aside His original form
and entered into the form of a man, being in the likeness of
man and the same as man. Therefore, He is able to touch the
heart of man.

God's coming to be a man, Jesus, was not like that of a
stage performer, who comes merely as an act. Rather, He was

in the womb of Mary, remaining there for nine months. After being born, according to the human manner He lived in the home of a poor carpenter in Nazareth for thirty years. We cannot imagine what kind of living that was. After thirty years, He began to carry out His ministry, like the Old Testament priests who needed to reach the age of thirty in order to be qualified to serve God. During that period of time, as Philippians 2:8 says, He was found in fashion as a man. Luke 19:10 says, "The Son of Man has come"; it does not say, "The Son of God has come" or "God has come." What did the Son of Man come to accomplish? He came "to seek and to save that which is lost."

THE LORD SENDING MEN
TO SEEK THE SONS OF PEACE

Luke 10:1 says, "Now after these things, the Lord appointed seventy others and sent them two by two before His face into every city and place where He Himself was about to come." Being in the flesh, the Lord could not go to every place at once. Therefore, He sent seventy others to go to the places to which He wanted to go. In the same way, when we go door-knocking today, every house that we visit is a place to which the Lord wants to go. The Lord has become the life-giving Spirit, the Spirit of power, and the Spirit of authority, but if such a Spirit were to knock on doors Himself, He would frighten people. Therefore, He must be in us, put us on, and send us out.

What do we go out to do? We go out to seek and to save that which is lost. These lost ones were chosen and predestinated by God before the foundation of the world. Those who are chosen and predestinated are the sons of peace (v. 6). All those who have knocked on doors have experienced this. Sometimes when you have knocked on someone's door, you may have felt that this person is not a son of peace, but after a few minutes you became clear that he indeed is a son of peace. Our going is to seek out the sons of peace. The Lord said to the disciples whom He sent, "Go; behold, I send you as lambs in the midst of wolves" (v. 3). Although the Lord sent the disciples as lambs in the midst of wolves, there were sons of peace among the wolves. Today He wants us to go to gain the sons of peace.

The desire of the Lord is for man to be saved. When He was on earth, He sent people out. After He departed from the world in His ascension, He said to His disciples, "All authority has been given to Me in heaven and on earth. Go therefore and disciple all the nations" (Matt. 28:18-19). This indicates that the Lord wants the disciples to go and seek out the sons of peace so that they may be regenerated and enter into the kingdom of the heavens. Those people were originally the people of Satan's kingdom, but through our seeking and preaching they are regenerated and become the people of God's kingdom. To find people in this way is to bring back the sons of peace.

On the other hand, this shows us that God does not want us to give messages in a big congregation, nor does He want us to ask people to come to hear messages. Rather, God wants us to go out. What shall we go out to do? We should go out to visit people. This is what the Lord Jesus did as the Son of Man, seeking and saving that which was lost. In the same way, our going door-knocking is to visit people in order to seek and to save that which is lost. Moreover, the Lord Jesus said to His disciples that when they entered someone's house, they should not say anything at first except, "Peace to this house" (Luke 10:5). When we were in Shanghai, we had two gospel tracts entitled "Where Are You?" and "Peace Be to You." The first time we went to visit people, we gave them "Where Are You?" Then the next time we went to visit them, we gave them "Peace Be to You." "Peace be to you" indicates that we are seeking the sons of peace. If someone is worthy to have peace, he is a son of peace, and peace will rest upon him. But if he is not worthy, the peace will return to us. Therefore, we should simply go.

We go out to seek the sons of peace because the Lord Himself wants us to go. He said that if people receive us, they receive Him (v. 16). We are representing the Lord when we go. Therefore, our going must be the Lord going with us and our going with the Lord. It is not that we go on our own to the place we choose. Our going is actually the Lord going with us to the place He wants to go. Therefore, we must be one with the Lord. We must be those who abide in the Lord and who let the Lord abide in us.

BEING WITH THE LORD, LIVING WITH THE LORD, AND BEARING FRUIT WITH THE LORD

Only when we are with the Lord and live with the Lord can we bear fruit with Him. The way branches bear fruit is by remaining with the tree and living with the tree. In the past we pursued to be spiritual, holy, and victorious, and many times we seemed to be quite spiritual, holy, and victorious, yet we did not bear fruit. Therefore, there are some problems with this kind of pursuit. As some saints have testified, if we go out to knock on doors but do not see anyone saved, this is a sign, an indication, that we have a problem either with God or with man. We must repent and confess our sins quickly. If we confess our sins, the next time we go door-knocking, we will have fruit immediately. Therefore, we must be fully joined to the Lord as one, practically living in Him and letting Him live in us. When we two—He and we, we and He—become one, our going out will be His going out. When we arrive at this stage, we will experience being full of authority.

In the past when we preached the gospel in our traditional way, we did not have this experience. As a result, not many people were saved. This was because we did not abide in Him. Our abiding in the Lord and going door-knocking to visit people is the Lord Jesus' seeking and saving that which is lost. It is not we who go door-knocking, but Jesus Christ who abides in us goes door-knocking in order to seek and to save that which is lost. Paul said, "I am crucified with Christ; and it is no longer I who live, but it is Christ who lives in me" (Gal. 2:20). Did Paul live Christ so that he might be spiritual, holy, and victorious? No, he lived Christ so that he might bear fruit. This is the meaning of 1 Timothy 1:15, which says, "Christ Jesus came into the world to save sinners." Since Paul lived Christ, he was the same as Christ in the matter of saving sinners.

I hope that we all would see that in order to be truly spiritual, holy, and victorious, we must abide in the Lord and also let Him abide in us. Whether or not we abide in the Lord is fully indicated by whether or not we bear fruit. If we do not bear fruit, this proves that we have not been abiding in the Lord and that there are some problems in our organic union with Him. This can be likened to the circulation of electricity in our homes. The electric current is cut off wherever there is insulation. Although the power station is functioning and the electric lamps are in place, if the supply of electricity is blocked, the lamps will not shine. Similarly, if we do not abide in the Lord, although outwardly we may still go to the meetings and keep ourselves from sin, we are insulated within and cut off from the Lord. This is why the Lord said, "He who abides in Me and I in him, he bears much fruit; for apart from Me you can do nothing" (John 15:5). This means that if we are apart from the Lord, we cannot bear fruit.

Every one of us is a branch of Christ and should bear fruit. If we do not bear fruit, we should realize that there is a problem. If we have lived our Christian life for decades yet in all those years have not borne any fruit, this indicates that we have had certain problems all along. Whether or not we are spiritual can be determined by whether or not we bear fruit. If we are not spiritual, it will be hard for us to gain people through door-knocking. Do not think that knocking on doors to visit people is an easy matter. Those with experience know that it is not easy. However, if we are willing to pray seriously and properly join ourselves to the Lord, immediately there will be the results. The supply of "electricity" will come again. Although the flow of "electricity" has been cut off, it will now be recovered, and our contacting people will spontaneously be effective.

I am afraid that many of us have been living a life of not bearing fruit. This should not be the case. Frankly speaking, preaching the gospel to bring people to salvation is not as difficult as it was before; now the way is much easier. Recently two sisters from Denmark and Germany testified that they preached the gospel to the owner of a restaurant in Yang Ming Shan, and he immediately believed into the Lord Jesus. This shows us that gradually the earth will be filled with Christians. We do not have to expend all our effort to invite people to love feasts to hear the gospel, as we did in the past.

Many whom we invited did not come even after ten invitations, and eventually they became annoyed with us. It was hard to save anyone in the way we took in the past. However, it is much easier now to get someone saved.

Whether or not the preaching of the gospel is easy altogether depends on what kind of people we are. If we are the proper kind of people, it will be easy; if we are not, then preaching will not be easy. If someone is untrained as a cook, he will not have the skill or the boldness to kill a chicken even if he is given the right kind of knife. He is not the right kind of person to do that job. If someone is trained, however, he can do the job without much effort. When we are trained to preach the gospel, our rate of success is very high. Within only three days some of the saints have baptized more than seventy people. This was easy for them, but it is not always easy for others. Whether or not it is easy altogether depends on what kind of people we are. If we are the right kind of people, it is easy, but if we are not, it is difficult.

We must be trained to be experts in preaching the gospel and in bringing people to salvation so that we can bring whomever we meet to salvation. Never say that it is very easy. Perhaps when other people go out, they are able to bring whomever they meet to baptism. However, when we go out, we may not able to do it. Satan has his authority in man. If we do not pray thoroughly, Satan will not let go. When we tell someone that he should be baptized, he may be unwilling and not consent. This is because Satan will not let go of him. Only when we pray thoroughly will we have the power. This thorough prayer is like the work of a surgeon. Before performing surgery on a patient, a doctor must first sterilize everything to kill the germs. Only when everything is sterilized completely can the surgery begin. In principle, this is the kind of person we must be. One who knocks on doors and brings people to salvation is one who is truly spiritual, holy, and victorious. This is a test of whether or not we are spiritual, victorious, and holy. If it is not easy for us to bring people to salvation, this proves that we are not truly spiritual, holy, and victorious. The matter of fruit-bearing is a very good test of our spirituality.

SETTING A GOAL AND GOING DOOR-KNOCKING
IN ONE ACCORD

We must set a goal for our fruit-bearing. Then, according to the goal, we should stretch forth with our full strength and pray before the Lord. I believe that the Lord will surely listen to our prayer. A young sister testified that originally she had decided to gain ten people, but eventually she gained only eight. In general we may feel that this was good enough. However, she felt that it was not right and that she must have some problems. When she went home, she prayed and confessed her sins before the Lord. After confessing her sins, she even prayed, "Lord, tomorrow You have to add four more to me to complement the two I yet lack." Such a prayer pleases God. In addition to prayer, whether or not our estimate and goal can be attained depends entirely on whether we endeavor. If we endeavor, they can surely be attained; if we do not endeavor, they certainly cannot be attained. Our estimate and goal can never be attained if we are loose. In the matter of door-knocking and visiting, we should stretch forth with our full strength.

This is the principle according to which God wanted Gideon to test the three hundred men (Judg. 7:2-8). Among the children of Israel there were many who wanted to fight against the enemy, but God told Gideon that the people were too many and that only three hundred would be sufficient. But how should they be selected? There was a very good way, which was to observe the manner in which they drank water. Some people came to the water and bowed down on their knees to drink it. God told Gideon that he should not accept these; they cared too much for the drinking of water. He could take only those who lapped the water with their tongue. Their heart was not on drinking the water; it was desperate to go out to fight against the Midianites and cast them out. This illustrates that once we set our goal, we cannot be loose. Not only do we need to pray more, but we also need to be more in one accord. Everything has to be intensified. In this way we will certainly be weighty. Once we are weighty and girded up, our goal will be attained.

THE SECRET FOR A CHRISTIAN
TO BE SPIRITUAL, HOLY, AND VICTORIOUS

The new way of going out to knock on doors, bring people to salvation, and baptize them is not an easy one. Rather, it is the secret of the saints' being spiritual, holy, and victorious. Taking this way will make the church holy and sanctified before the Lord, and the saints will be built up together. In the past we listened to many messages concerning being built up, but the result was still that everyone built up his own matters. No one was attuned to another one. As a result there was not much reality of the building or any great result in our work. Now we have this proper way. Therefore, we should "go" in one accord, knocking on doors, visiting people, bringing them to salvation, actively taking care of home meetings, building ourselves up, and being built up with the saints.

We all must have a thorough dealing with the Lord and be thoroughly cleansed to be without any problems so that He can pass through our inward being. We and He, He and we, must have the unhindered relationship of the "power station" and the "lamps," in which we are fully connected and the "electricity" freely flows. This matters not only for our bearing fruit; it matters even more for our progress in the spiritual life.

(A message given on February 24, 1987 in Taipei, Taiwan)

CHAPTER FOUR

HOW TO PERFECT THE HOME MEETINGS

Building and perfecting the home meetings are the key to the success of the practice of the new way. The following are some important points that can help us build up and perfect the home meetings.

PRAYING, CONFESSING, ASKING FOR CLEANSING, AND BEING FILLED

First of all, we must prepare ourselves before going out to visit people. This preparation is nothing less than prayer. Prayer is indispensable in our Christian service. Before serving in any aspect, we must first pray, confess, and ask to be cleansed and filled. If we do not first pray, our going to visit people in a hasty way will definitely be futile. We must have some good prayer before we can go out to fight the spiritual battle, asking the Lord to cleanse and to fill us.

EXERCISING AND USING OUR SPIRIT

Next, we must exercise our spirit. We human beings have three parts—spirit, soul, and body. Because of man's fall, the common people can use only two parts, which are their soul and body. However, since we Christians are regenerated in our spirit, we should exercise our spirit. The most important thing in our preaching the gospel and serving the Lord is for us to use our spirit. Although the activity of our body is involved in every kind of service, and the soul also must be in its function, the most important and crucial part is still our spirit. Therefore, we must learn to exercise and follow the spirit.

Some may ask, "How do I know that the spirit is leading

me within? How do I know if I am following the spirit?" We
may not know what it is to be in spirit, but we certainly know
what it is to not be in spirit. For instance, when we are about
to lose our temper, or when we have already lost our temper,
then we are certain that we have not been in spirit and that
our actions were not out from the spirit. Then what is it to
follow the spirit? Simply speaking, to follow the spirit is to not
do what we sense is not of the spirit. Whatever we sense is not
of the spirit, we should not do. Now some may ask, "How can
we not do anything? If we don't do anything, nothing will
happen." For an unbeliever to not do that which is not of the
spirit means that nothing remains, because their spirit is not
in function. However, when we who serve the Lord pray and
then not do all the things that we sense are not of the spirit,
what remains is all of the spirit. This is very simple and clear.
After we pray, we must exercise our spirit wherever we go. As
to what we should say to people, we also have to exercise our
spirit. Whatever we feel that is not of the spirit, we should not
do it. Then the rest will all be of the spirit.

BEING DELIVERED FROM RELIGIOUS RITUALS

Moreover, we have to be delivered from religious rituals.
Since religious concepts have been planted deeply in man's
heart, the secular people regard Christianity as a kind of religion, thinking that Christianity is merely for people to worship
God. Therefore, if we want to establish a meeting in people's
homes after they are saved, they will think that we are leading
them to have a "Sunday service." They will see us as pastors
and preachers. The saints from abroad, in particular, will be
considered foreign missionaries. If we are not careful, we may
behave as if we were pastors. The new ones will then "ordain"
us and accept whatever we say. Then the more they accept us,
the happier we will be, and the happier we become, the more
we will be like pastors. As a result, a religious service will
come into being. We do not need to hang out a sign to tell
people that the church is special and is different from the
denominations, that we do not have pastors or any religious
rituals. It is useless merely to say these things. What is useful
is the way we conduct ourselves, how we talk and behave in

their homes. This is the most crucial pattern for the home meetings.

When we meet in the homes, we should never presumptuously tell people that we are there to teach them. We must not have any such presumption. Rather, we should simply be ordinary Christians who meet with them. The first thing we must do is break the heritage and tradition of holding "services" in the way of Christianity. After we come to someone's home, we should not first arrange the chairs as if we are going to have a Sunday service. The more the chairs are arranged in a normal way, the better it is. Never go and arrange the seats like someone who takes care of a chapel. In addition, do not choose a special seat for yourselves as the pastors do, and even the more, do not assume the responsibility of reading the Scriptures like the preachers do. Simply sit in a normal way in an ordinary seat. If after arriving in a home we feel the chairs are too messy, we busy ourselves arranging them, and then we choose a place to sit and call a hymn, we will successfully conduct a "Sunday service." Hence, we should never do these things.

Perhaps someone will ask, "If arranging seats makes us chapel keepers, calling hymns makes us pastors, praying makes us junior pastors, and reading the Scriptures makes us preachers, then what should we do in the home meetings?" The problem of religious concepts is the reason it is better not to prematurely bring the new ones to meet in the meeting hall. By bringing them too early they may soon be "contaminated," and the poison of religion will get into them. Since we have not been entirely delivered from the rituals and traditions of the old religion, we should not bring the newly saved ones to the meetings in the old way.

When it comes to the time in the home meetings that we usually call a hymn, it may be better not to call one. Rather, we may talk with them about their daily matters. We may ask them how many children they have, or whether they know what to do in a meeting. They may say that they do not know, or they may know only a little. No matter how they answer, we can take the opportunity to fellowship with them about walking by the spirit. We should not be like those who learn to box according to rigid rules about which punch to use first and which to use second. Blindly following a set pattern is of little effect.

After leading them in this way one or two times, they will have learned something. Then when we visit them the third time, we can say, "Brother, what should we do now?" The new one may say, "Let's pray." We may ask him, "Who should pray?" If he says, "You should pray," we can tell him, "Brother, I don't want to be a pastor. I don't want to pray first. Perhaps you can pray." Gradually, we have to let them know that a meeting is not a matter of forms or rituals but a matter of following the spirit. Although we may have set the meeting time for 7:30 P.M., we may not need to wait until then to start the meeting. This is a meeting in their home. After they finish dinner at 6:45 P.M. and are cleaning up together, the little brother can pray to begin the meeting while the mother is still washing the dishes. Then the older brother can sing, "We need Jesus, we need Jesus." In this way the home meeting begins.

If we practice this from the beginning of a home meeting, we can break the concept of having a Sunday service. It is not necessary to start the meeting by reading the Word or by praying. It is not even a requirement to start the meeting at a fixed time. The meeting may not begin in the living room; it may simply begin in the kitchen. After finishing dinner, while it is still early, someone can wash the dishes and sing, "Since Jesus came into my heart." Then the young son in the next room may echo, "Amen, hallelujah!" In this way the meeting can begin. Let them know that there are no forms or rituals in the meetings. There is only the Spirit, only the presence of the Lord. If we understand home meetings to this extent, then when we go and help the home meetings, we can bring people to be delivered from religion. This is the way to break the tradition of Christianity, and this is also the new way and living way we must take.

In the meetings, regardless of whether the new ones are reading verses, giving a testimony, or speaking something, do not correct them. If there is definitely something improper, adjust them privately, or wait until the next time. Never correct them on the spot, because this will quench their spirit and ordinances will then come in. If a point comes when they do not do anything, we may then lead them a little by asking, "Should we read some verses now?" Then we can ask them where we should read. Perhaps we have decided to read Revelation, but they want to read Genesis. We should not say no. Rather, we should read Genesis with them. After reading, we can explain it to them a little. Then we can ask them to tell us why they wanted to read this portion. In this way they will know how to read the Bible, how to share, and how to give a testimony. There are many ways to practice, but it is sufficient if we can grasp the principle.

However, this does not mean that we should forget about our burden. After they have met for fifteen to twenty minutes, and after they all have learned a little, we can, in the form of fellowship, suggest a portion of the Bible according to our burden. After reading it, we should not speak immediately. We can ask them whether this portion is good. For example, the portion we read may be John 1:29: "Behold, the Lamb of God, who takes away the sin of the world!" We may ask them, "Is this portion of the Word good? Which phrase is the best? Which point is the best?" This is to inspire them, and in this inspiring we can release our burden to them. Finally, we can lead everyone to memorize the verse. If we help the home meeting in this way, the new ones will not think that we have come to conduct a Sunday service with them. Although we do not need a certain pattern, we must have a definite burden within. Nevertheless, we should not bother too much about what we need to do. We should simply give them an impression in a flexible way that we are going there to have fellowship with them.

EXPLAINING THE NEED, THE PURPOSE, AND THE PRACTICE OF THE MEETING

In the first home meeting, we should talk about our need to meet. We can tell the new ones that Christians are like sheep, possessing a communal nature. Christians are also like bees, which swarm together. In truth, all human beings possess a communal nature, as the ancient Chinese used to say, "To be human is to be communal." No matter how many blessings a man has or how much wealth he possesses, he would never be willing to live in seclusion in the mountains and not come down for three years. It is not human nature to live alone apart from the human community. However, today society is full of sins. It is right to be communal, but the problem is how to be communal and with whom we should be communal. If someone joins himself to the wrong group of people, he will be defiled. If we join ourselves to mah-jongg players, eventually we will be playing mah-jongg with them. If we join ourselves to those who take drugs, we will end up taking drugs with them. This is the meaning of another Chinese saying: "Whoever touches vermilion turns red; whoever touches ink turns black." Therefore, we can see that the best community is the Christian meetings. The Christian meetings give people the joy of gathering together. This is the noblest, purest, and most profitable joy. To illustrate further, a piece of charcoal cannot burn by itself; if it were to burn, it would go out very quickly. Rather, it has to burn with other pieces of charcoal to make a bright fire.

Matthew 18:20 says, "For where there are two or three gathered into My name, there am I in their midst." We have to tell the new ones that in every meeting the Lord is with us and that He is in our midst. If we want to enjoy the Lord's presence, we have to meet. We need to speak these basic points into them.

Acts 2:42-47 tells us that the first purpose of our meeting is to learn and continue steadfastly in the apostles' teaching and to come together to have fellowship, to break bread, and to pray. At the same time, we can also teach others and preach the gospel. These are the purposes of meeting. Besides this, Hebrews 10:24 says that we have to consider one another so as to incite one another to love. This also is a purpose of the Christian meetings. Hence, the purpose of the Christian meetings is severalfold.

The Bible reveals not only one way to meet but many ways. There are home meetings and meetings of the whole church coming together. There are big meetings and also small meetings. These are according to the practical situation and need.

In the church in Taipei first there are meetings in individual homes. These are the smallest, most fundamental, and most basic kind. Second, there are group meetings in which several homes come together. Third, there are district meetings in which several groups come together in a meeting hall. Sometimes there are medium-sized meetings of several districts coming together. In addition, there are corporate meetings of all the saints in Taipei and even meetings in which the church in Taipei meets with the churches in other cities. Occasionally there are meetings for the whole island of Taiwan and even international conferences on a larger scale.

The way to meet is nothing other than to listen to God's speaking, read the Scriptures, sing hymns, pray, give testimonies, encourage one another, preach the gospel, and so on. We have to tell the new ones a little about all of this. Nevertheless, whatever we speak when we lead a home meeting, it should not be long. We should always allow time for others to speak something, and we should teach them how to speak in the meetings. We should tell them that when they speak in the meetings, they are speaking to others not to themselves, so they should speak loud enough for people to hear them. We should let them know these things in the first or second meeting.

TERMINATING THE PAST

In this way we can fellowship with them that for a Christian to worship God and to serve and follow the Lord after his salvation, he has to terminate his past. Before we were saved, we made many mistakes in our daily life that left some consequences which need to be dealt with. Apart from this, we may have some improper items in our house such as idols, which should also be cleared up. In the Bible there are two excellent examples that speak concerning the termination of the past. One is in Luke 19, which talks about Zaccheus, who was originally a tax collector who constantly defrauded those who paid taxes. After he was saved, however, he immediately said to the Lord Jesus, "If I have taken anything from anyone by false accusation, I restore four times as much" (v. 8). Another example is in Acts 19:19-20, which tells us that after the Ephesians were saved, they brought their demonic books together and burned them.

After we are saved, there are certain things in our home that need to be cleared up. The first thing is idols. The second are gambling devices, such as cards and mah-jongg. Third, there are the items used for drinking alcohol, and the fourth are the items used for smoking. The fifth is anything related to dragons. In the Bible the dragon clearly refers to Satan. After we are saved, we want to follow the Lord and take His way. Therefore, all these things which offend God and are not pleasing to Him should be dealt with so that we will have a good testimony before man, joy in ourselves, and no barriers when we pray. This is especially true in the home meetings. All the furniture and decorations in a home should show people that we are of Christ Jesus. All these things are what a saved one will gradually do and should do before the Lord under His leading.

LEARNING TO USE *LIFE LESSONS* AND *TRUTH LESSONS*

We need to learn to use *Life Lessons,* but not in a rigid way. There are twelve lessons in each volume. It is not necessary for us to read one lesson every time we meet. We may cover one lesson in two sessions, or we may cover two lessons at one time. Our way does not need to be rigid. It is sufficient simply to see the main points; we do not need to bring up other points until later. After using *Life Lessons,* we also should learn to use *Truth Lessons. Truth Lessons* is written in a coherent and systematic way and can be considered as the essence of the basic teaching for a new believer. It has not only outlines and main points but also the content to explain the outlines and main points in a concise and clear way. Therefore, it is very practical.

LEARNING TO ANSWER QUESTIONS WHEN USING *TRUTH LESSONS*

When we go to the home meetings, we will always encounter the practical problems of the new ones, which we cannot ignore. In order to take care of their problems, we may not be able to use *Truth Lessons* step by step, lesson by lesson.

Sometimes we may have to put it aside for the time being and concentrate on dealing with the problems. However, we must take care that when we answer the questions of new believers, regardless of what they ask, giving simpler answers is always better. Do not expect them to understand everything. Everyone who has children knows that no matter what kind of questions children ask, the questions are endless. Even three days and nights are not enough to answer all their questions. The more we answer them, the more they like to ask. As a result, the questions can go on endlessly.

We should deal with the new believers in the same way. For example, someone may ask whether or not they should worship their ancestors. We can answer them in this way: The way to care for your ancestors is simply to honor and remember them, and the best and highest way to honor and remember them is to behave well and live a proper human life, even as the ancient Chinese sages said, "To live a proper human life is to honor your ancestors." It is best to answer this question only to this extent. If the new believer asks further, "Should we worship the ancestors?", then we should say, "If your parents do, then do not argue with them. Regarding other questions you may have, we can talk about them later."

Sometimes they may ask positive questions. When they pray, for example, they may sense some hindrances within them. To ask about this is to ask a good question. We should take this opportunity to speak a little to them to let them know that to pray is to come near to the Lord. At the same time, to pray is also to exercise the spirit. The spirit is the organ for us to contact the Lord. In our living we may talk and act in a light way without caring for the sense in our spirit, and we may not sense the obstacles and hindrances in our spirit. However, when we quiet ourselves and pray with our spirit, the spirit gains ground in us, and we then become very clear about the feeling of the spirit. Then whenever something is wrong in our spirit, we sense the barrier. Most of the time this barrier is our sins or our disobedience in some matter before God. Therefore, we have to confess our sins immediately, one after another, until there are no more barriers within. To answer a question in this way will make a very good home meeting. If the new ones have no questions, we can read *Truth Lessons* with them. This is a very convenient and flexible way.

The best way to teach *Truth Lessons,* simply speaking, is not to read the lessons together with them but to read the outlines at the beginning of every lesson, giving some explanation while reading. Before reading with them, we have to read it ourselves and understand the general idea and the main points of the chapter. Then we can help them when we read with them. I believe that after they read the message, they will find it very meaningful. *Truth Lessons* will be published in four levels, with four volumes in each level. Its content is very rich. If the new ones can receive some solid education in *Life Lessons* and *Truth Lessons,* they will surely be remaining fruit.

THE SECRET FOR THE SUCCESS OF THE NEW WAY

The success of the new way hinges on two key points. The first one is getting people saved and baptized. The second is the home meetings to keep the saved ones in the church life so that they can be remaining fruit and be perfected to be useful vessels. If a local church truly takes the new way, it will begin with a fourfold increase in number each year. Where there is originally one hundred saints, after one year there should be four hundred. Three hundred out of this number will be newly added to the church life, and one-fourth of these three hundred should be remaining fruit. Hence, there should be two hundred who meet regularly by the end of the year.

Simply speaking, at least one-fourth of all who are baptized by us should remain and have home meetings. Last year we baptized eight thousand people in addition to the four thousand baptized at the start of our full-time training. This totals twelve thousand. Of these twelve thousand, there should still be three thousand who remain. According to past experience, among these three thousand remaining ones there should be five or six hundred homes in which they break bread. If five or six meet in each home to break bread, about five hundred homes are needed for this purpose. These are only the newly saved ones; this does not include those who already meet in the church.

Therefore, the key for the home meetings is first to keep one-fourth of the newly baptized ones. Second, five percent of these remaining ones should serve full time. Apart from this, twenty-five percent should be going out for door-knocking every week. The home meetings are considered successful only if these three things are fulfilled. If not, we cannot reach our estimates for the increase. We cannot look only at the outward situation of the number of people who are baptized and the good condition of the home meetings. We must realize that this is not enough. We have to keep our eyes on our estimates and our goal. Full-timers need to be produced, and one-fourth of the saints must be raised up to go door-knocking every week. This requires all of us to endeavor together.

(A message given on February 26, 1987 in Taipei, Taiwan)

CHAPTER FIVE

PERFECTING AND STRENGTHENING THE HOME MEETINGS

BEING JOINED TO THE LORD AS ONE SPIRIT

We all know that to do anything requires real power. When we go to perfect a home meeting, the real power lies in our being joined to the Lord as one spirit. Whether or not we are joined to the Lord as one spirit is spontaneously revealed in our living in several ways. First, we must be people who always pray and fellowship with the Lord. This does not mean we need to pray for many things. Often when we have too many things to pray for, they become a distraction to our being joined to the Lord. According to the New Testament, to pray unceasingly means that we are always joined to the Lord and that we keep contacting the Lord in our inner being. As a result, our entire being is filled with and occupied by the Lord inwardly, and our outward, spontaneous expression is thanksgiving and praises.

In Ephesians 5 Paul charged the believers to not be drunk with wine. Then he said, "But be filled in spirit" (v. 18). The result of being filled in spirit is to be filled with the word of the Lord. Our mouths not only speak and sing the word of the Lord unceasingly, but they are also full of thanksgiving and praises (vv. 19-20). This requires us to be people who live in the Lord and are joined to the Lord continually.

If we are too formal and rigid when we lead a home meeting, we will definitely kill the meeting. These formal and rigid ways may not be wrong, but they do not issue in the living out of the divine life. We must be people who are joined to the Lord in our spirit. This kind of joining to the Lord will make our expression fresh, living, and touching, and our expression

will cause others to feel that we are people full of vitality. If a
person weeps in front of us, even though we may not weep, we
will still feel a certain sorrow. When a weeping person comes
to us, he makes us want to weep. On the contrary, if a joyful
person comes to us, even though we may not want to laugh,
we still will laugh. A laughing person, one who brings laughter with him, causes us to respond with laughter. The kind of
person we are determines the kind of response we produce.

When we go to perfect a home meeting, we need to bring
the Lord with us. The Lord is lively, fresh, full of vitality, and
always joyful. Of course, the Bible tells us that the Lord Jesus
had times of grief and sorrow, and in Genesis 6:6, when man
was corrupted to the uttermost, God grieved and repented
that He had made man on the earth. It is true that God has
times of sorrow, but we do not see many instances in the Bible
in which God grieves. Rather, God is continually joyful. God is
not a sorrowful God but a joyful God. Today since we are
joined to God and are one spirit with the Lord, we should be a
joyful and released people.

It is right for us to be proper, but we should not be too
restrained. If we are released, joyful, lively, and fresh, when
we go to a home meeting, we will bring with us these sweet
qualities. A Japanese has the look of a Japanese; when he
goes to a home meeting, he brings the Japanese culture and
atmosphere with him. Likewise, when an American goes to a
home meeting, he brings an American atmosphere, and if a
five-year-old child goes there, he brings a naughty atmosphere.
Therefore, when we go to perfect a home meeting, the most
important key is the kind of person we are. A Japanese will
"perfect" a Japanese home meeting, an American will create
an American home meeting, and a joking person will produce
a joking home meeting. Similarly, a formal and rigid person
will produce a dead and cold home meeting. We cannot pretend. The kind of person we are is the kind of home meeting
we will produce. How useful we are in the Lord's hand and
the kind of home meeting we can produce all depend on the
extent, the degree, and the condition of our joining to the Lord.
If the extent of our joining to the Lord is great, the degree is

high, and the condition is good, the home meeting we lead will certainly be a good one.

We all know that to do a certain thing requires a certain kind of person. When a surgeon is about to operate, he must be completely sterile, and his hair and body must be covered. Only then can he perform the surgery. If a surgeon does not cleanse his hands and cover his head, he will unconsciously spread the bacteria on his body to the patient. When we go to perfect a home meeting, we often unintentionally bring our old man to the saints. Our original intention is to bring the Lord Jesus to them, but often the Lord Jesus does not come. Instead, a Japanese, an American, or a joking person comes. Although we intend to bring the Lord, it is questionable who eventually comes.

It is certainly easy to change outward things. It is easy to ask a surgeon to wash his hands and to sterilize and cover his whole body. However, it is very difficult for a person to change his nature. There is a proverb that says, "Changing one's nature is more difficult than moving mountains and rivers." Some co-workers who were trained more than thirty years ago still do not have much change. Even up until today they are what they were. When a person has been molded into a certain form, he cannot be changed when the east wind comes, nor can he be changed when the west wind comes. He is the same way in the summer, and he is still the same way in the winter. When others feel cold, he is not cold; when others feel hot, he is not hot. When others weep, he has almost no feeling; when others laugh, he does not laugh. When you lift your hands to sing hymns and be joyful with this kind of person, he does not respond, and when you want to pray aloud with him, he does not make a sound. No matter how one may rebuke this kind of person, he does not become angry. With great strength he seems as invincible and stable as a great mountain; he cannot be moved.

If this kind of person goes to lead a home meeting or a church meeting, the whole meeting will be as dead and rigid as he is. Not a single person in the church under his leading will be beside himself for the Lord. Since such a one is not beside himself, he certainly cannot lead a "crazy" meeting or perfect others to be beside themselves. However hard one tries, he cannot ignite a fire in this kind of person. It seems he is fireproof, even fire extinguishing. This shows us that in the matter of perfecting a home meeting, the most difficult one to deal with is ourselves.

We have to be adjusted before the Lord and not remain in our old nature. Whether we are Shantongese, Cantonese, Japanese, or American, we have to remember this principle: We saved ones have "moved our home" from Adam into Christ. The phrase *in Christ* is a great one, but few people have the actual experience of being in Christ in their practice. This experience is in the spirit. The Bible does not say that he who is joined to the Lord is one Christ with Him, but that he who is joined to the Lord is one spirit (1 Cor. 6:17). This is altogether a matter of the spirit. Therefore, we must learn not to stay in our own person but to enter into the spirit and be joined to the Lord in spirit. In the past we used only our mind to think, our emotion to manage things, and our strong will to decide. This demonstrates that we were people who stayed in our soul and remained in our self. We must learn to walk not by the parts of our soul but by our spirit, always turning back to our spirit. Once we turn to our spirit, we contact the Lord, and our spirit is fanned into flame and burning.

In the New Testament there are two passages that speak of being burning and fervent in spirit. One is in Romans 12:11: "Be burning in spirit, serving the Lord." The other is in Acts 18:25, which speaks of Apollos. Although he had little revelation and did not know much truth, he was fervent in spirit. In common speech there is no such expression as being fervent in spirit; we mainly speak of emotional impulses. However, if a Christian is emotionally impulsive, he will fail, because to be emotionally impulsive is in the self, the natural man, and even the flesh. Therefore, we must be ones who are fervent in spirit.

Before going to perfect a home meeting, we ourselves must first have a transfer from our soul—our mind, emotion, and will—into our spirit. This requires our exercise. We need to go out and labor, but we should never forget that before we go to a home, we must first have a transfer. This transfer is to move quickly from our mind into our spirit. We may be in our spirit one moment, but in the next moment we may run to our mind. Therefore, we have to move back. We must resolve not to go to perfect a home meeting before we turn back to our spirit. Every time we go to a home meeting, we have to be in our spirit. Moreover, when we go to the home meeting to fellowship and speak with others, we need to be careful, because it is easy for us to unconsciously move back to our "old home," our soul. This is the way we need to exercise.

BEING PROFICIENT IN THE WORD OF THE LORD

Second, we must be proficient in the word of the Lord. Being proficient implies not only being experienced but also being familiar with and skilled in a certain thing. The word of the Lord is the word of life. Not only should we understand it, but we also need to enter into it. When we enter into the word of the Lord and experience this word, we will be proficient in the word. For this purpose, we need to read more of the Bible and the spiritual publications. The more we read the word of the Lord, the more we will experience the Lord's word and the more proficient and skillful we will be. Then when we go to perfect a home meeting, the element of the Lord's word will come out whenever we open our mouth. The Lord's word is the expression of the Lord. The coming out of the element of the Lord's word is the Lord in us being expressed through our speaking. This is not our own speaking but the spontaneous flow of the Lord's word.

We may illustrate this with a person's education. If a person has graduated only from elementary school, his manner of speaking will give him away. If he has graduated from high school, his manner of speaking will certainly be different. If he continues his studies through college, his speaking will be even more different. Such a person will have been educated for many years and saturated with the words of his learning throughout these years. Moreover, he will have continually practiced these words and become familiar with them. As a result, he will be skillful and proficient in these words. A person simply needs to open his mouth to speak, and others will know the kind of education he has received. Those who are not educated scold others in a certain way, while those who are educated scold others in a different way. A person cannot pretend; one person's constitution is not the same as another's.

We must be continually exercised in the word of the Lord. In Hebrews 5:13 Paul mentions the word of righteousness, and in Hebrews 6:5 he speaks of the good word. The good word is the word of grace. The word of the Lord in the New Testament is of two categories: the good word, that is, the word of grace, and the word of righteousness. The good word, the word of grace, is easy to understand. According to Hebrews, it refers to the word of the Lord's earthly ministry, which is recorded in the four Gospels. Today most Christians treasure only the word in the four Gospels. The word in the four Gospels is truly good, but it is only the good word, the word of grace, and is still not the word of righteousness. When Paul wrote Hebrews, he spoke about the word of the Lord's heavenly ministry, which is excellent, deep, and mysterious; this is the word of righteousness. When we go to perfect a home meeting, we need to be familiar with these two kinds of word.

To apply for a good job in any field today generally requires a person to be at least a college graduate. If a person has not graduated from college, it is usually not easy for him to find a good job because his practical knowledge is not adequate. He must pass through certain courses in order to be fitted for his job. At the same time, his mind will become skillful. In this way, regardless of the circumstances he is put into, whatever he does will be done well. Sixty years ago we might have looked down on an electrician who digs through walls, pulls cables, and repairs wires. Not everyone may realize that in America a person needs to graduate at least from high school and then receive specialized training for two years to do this work, because this job is technically and scientifically specialized. Likewise, some people may think that serving the Lord is an easy matter. Little do they know that serving the Lord requires us to be skillful in all things.

Everyone who has the heart to love and serve the Lord must spend time in His word. When I first started to serve the Lord, I spent more than half my time each day in studying the word of the Lord. I spent more than half of each day to study, search, record, and copy the word, and this became a great help to me in my later days. Therefore, apart from the necessary time for working, eating, sleeping, and exercising, the remainder of our time should be spent diligently reading the Bible and the spiritual publications. If we want to be skillful in this aspect, we need to exercise ourselves. This is not the work of a day, nor the work of a year; it is the work of a lifetime. Whenever we have time, we need to seize the opportunity to study the Bible. We have to read through the Bible at least once in a year. In addition, we should read all of our spiritual publications once. We must be ones who are equipped with the truth. Then when we go out, we will spontaneously have the strength to perfect others.

BEING BURNING IN SPIRIT

Third, when we go to perfect a home meeting, we must be burning in spirit. Being burning in spirit is the morale among us. If a brother and a sister in the training get married, for example, we will all be joyful. However, we need to consider practically whether it is appropriate for trainees to get married during the term of training. Will this affect the morale? The training is to ignite and fan the flame within us. We are fanning every day. Just when the fire is fanned into flame, a marriage may be "cold water" poured on us, and our morale will diminish. Then when we go door-knocking, we may have no power because we are not burning in spirit.

We hope that all the trainees will delay their marriage plans until their training is over so that they can consecrate all their time for the training and the morale of the training will not be affected. In the age of the judges in the Old Testament, there were more than thirty thousand who heard the trumpets of Gideon and came to join the army, but God said there were too many, and He tested them by the way they drank water. Those who knelt down to drink the water, God rejected. Instead, God accepted those who remained ready to fight as they lapped the water. He needed that kind of people. Although there were only three hundred of these, they were able to fight (Judg. 7:2-7). This was their morale. When we go to perfect a home meeting, we must have such a morale.

When many newly saved young people see the trainees serving full time while they are so young, they have the same desire within them. This is the morale that compels others to be the same way. The traditional work of preaching in Christianity has no effect because it does not have any morale. Those who become preachers think that to take up a career of preaching is simply to bring a few people to the Sunday service; if they can do this, their mission is fulfilled. There is no morale in this practice. Today we who serve the Lord are not only volunteer soldiers but also desperate fighters who serve at the risk of our lives. In this way the morale is generated among us.

However, this kind of morale cannot be pretended. If we are not this kind of people, when we go to perfect a home meeting, we will not have much impact. However, if we are this kind of people, when we go to perfect a home meeting, every member of the family will be perfected. A certain elderly grandmother who had worshipped Buddha for her whole life never expected that her granddaughter would believe in the Lord and be saved. Although she loved this granddaughter, it was not easy for such an elderly person to leave the idols she worshipped. This granddaughter had a fiancé who was burning in spirit, and he talked to the grandmother about believing in the Lord. After a short while she also believed in the Lord and was baptized in the bathtub in her home. Then right away she burned all her idols which she had worshipped for decades. This demonstrates our morale. When we go to someone's home to perfect the meeting there, we need to have this kind of morale by which others can see that we belong to Jesus, that for us to live is Jesus, and that all we think and everything within us is nothing but Jesus. Once we have such a morale, even though we may not speak much, others will be benefitted. This is the morale we need to have.

BEING SOBERMINDED
AND NOT FRIVOLOUS IN CHARACTER

The three foregoing matters are for our fanning people into flame, causing them to be burning in spirit. However, when we are zealous, it is easy to be frivolous. The Bible tells us that we need to be soberminded. Those who serve the Lord should not be frivolous. When we go to perfect a home meeting, although we should not be rigid, neither should we be playful. Rather, we should be dignified. The term *soberminded* is difficult to explain. In Titus 1:8 the Chinese Union Version translates this phrase as "grave," while the Recovery Version translates it as "of a sober mind," meaning having a mind of soberness, being sober and self-disciplined. A person who is muddled cannot be grave. If a person is casual and muddled, laughing when he should not laugh and crying when he should not cry, he is frivolous and not soberminded. We need to be clear in our mind and of a sober mind.

We may illustrate sobermindedness in the following way. If you are in your own room, you can lie on your bed. However, when you come to someone else's living room, you may find the couch comfortable and lie down. Then when he comes and sees you, you may still not get up. Rather, you may say, "Brother, I am so joyful that the grace of the Lord is sufficient." Acting in this way will surely make others think you are abnormal. If we are dignified and of a sober mind, we will behave properly and sobermindedly, having a proper expression in every aspect. Hence, the term *soberminded* has the meaning of soberness, self-control, and self-discipline. When we are alone in our room, whether or not we have self-control may not be apparent, but when we are in someone's living room, we should behave in a soberminded way.

After speaking of being soberminded, Titus 1:8 says, "Righteous, holy, self-controlled." In actuality, all these matters are related to being "of a sober mind." For us to have righteousness, holiness, and self-control, we must be people of a sober mind who can control ourselves, restrain ourselves, and give ourselves no ground to be loose. This should be so not only in big matters but even in small matters. To scratch our feet carelessly while we speak in a home meeting is to not behave out of a sober mind. A person of a sober mind should have righteousness, holiness, and self-control. A person who is soberminded and grave is a person who is not frivolous.

Not only so, a person who is grave and soberminded is clear in his mind and sharp in his vision. He perceives when he should laugh and when he should cry. He contacts elderly people in one way and young people in another way. He has one way towards men and another way towards women. When sisters go out to contact people and the host of a house turns out to be a man, they should keep a certain separation when they shake his hand. They should shake hands with a person of the same sex in one way and shake hands with a person of the opposite sex in another. This is to be grave. If someone contacts everyone in the same way with no difference at all, he is frivolous, not discerning the actual situation.

In your practice you should not pretend to be grave simply for the sake of a home meeting. Rather, you should exercise to be grave in your daily living. You should not pretend or be a muddled person. Instead, you should have a clear view, a sober mind, and a proper measure. To be of a sober mind means to have self-discipline, to be self-restrained, and to have self-control in everything. However, this is not to put on a lofty appearance, making people feel that we who serve the Lord are special. This is absolutely not true. We have to be weighty people who do not speak thoughtlessly, express our opinion casually, or convey our attitude lightly. Rather, we are fresh, living, and spontaneous. We stay within our limit and measure, our manner is appropriate, and our speaking and behavior are grave and fitting.

CONCERNING THE BREAKING OF BREAD

In practicing the new way, the breaking of bread is also an important issue. In the matter of bread-breaking, we have always been very cautious. In the past few decades, we never would hastily begin to break the bread in any place. However, because of the rigidity in certain areas of our former practice, the function of many saints has been annulled. Hence, we do not want to entirely follow our former old practice. Instead, we want to follow what the Bible says, allowing the church life to be practically carried out and built up in the homes of the newly saved ones. This will then bring in the breaking of bread, because bread-breaking is the most basic practice in the church life.

Being Cautious in Establishing
the Bread and the Cup

We still should be cautious in establishing the meeting for breaking bread. First, we should not be hasty to break bread in the home of a newly saved one. We must have much fellowship with him to understand his living, his environment, and his relationships with his relatives, friends, and neighbors. In this way we will know whether or not he has evil companions, such as companions in gambling, or whether he has other relationships which are unclean in his family life or with his neighbors, relatives, friends, and colleagues. A person may be saved and baptized, but his old living may not be cleared up, and there may be many matters which are wrong not only in the eyes of Christians but also in the eyes of the world. Before we have this kind of understanding, it is too hasty and absolutely not appropriate to establish a bread-breaking meeting in his home. We must know a person's situation and go to have fellowship with him week by week, leading him in a spontaneous way so that he can have the opportunity to clear up his old living.

The Clearance of the Old Living

Next, if there are still unclean things in his home, such as idols or a mah-jongg table, we need to help him clear those up. It is a terrible thing to establish a meeting for breaking bread in a person's home without first dealing with these matters. It may be that the table used for breaking the bread in the morning becomes a mah-jongg table in the evening. This would be a great loss to the Lord's testimony. Therefore, in such cases we need to have a careful observation and lead people to have a thorough clearance. Being influenced by the Ching Dynasty, Chinese people like to have dragons in their homes. In the Bible the dragon signifies Satan, but in Chinese society the dragon is regarded as something good. This is the stratagem of the evil one, and we need to pay attention to this.

After people are saved, they will spontaneously abhor unclean and sinful things because of Christ's life in them.

However, we still must help them gradually to have the proper knowledge concerning a thorough clearance of their living. In this way, we can begin breaking bread in their homes at the appropriate time. If at the beginning the number in a home is too small for bread-breaking, we can combine two to three neighboring homes for this meeting.

Fellowshipping concerning the Meaning of the Breaking of Bread

Furthermore, before breaking bread, we need to have fellowship with the new ones once or twice on the significance of bread-breaking. The first meaning of bread-breaking is the remembrance of the Lord. In 1 Corinthians 11:24-25 the Lord said, "This is My body, which is given for you; this do unto the remembrance of Me....This cup is the new covenant established in My blood; this do, as often as you drink it, unto the remembrance of Me." This clearly indicates the meaning of bread-breaking. It is not a religious ritual; rather, it is wholly for the remembrance of the Lord. Remembrance implies love, because we remember only those whom we love. It is precisely because we love the Lord that we consider Him and remember Him. According to the historical record, in the early days shortly after the Lord died, the believers broke bread on the Lord's Day every week for the remembrance of the Lord, as Acts 20:7 says, "And on the first day of the week, when we gathered together to break bread." Likewise, we need to break bread at least once a week for the remembrance of the Lord.

How do we remember the Lord? To speak simply, to remember the Lord is to eat and drink Him. To eat the bread is to eat the Lord, and to drink the cup is to drink the Lord. Whom are we drinking? We are drinking the Lord who has dispensed Himself into us through the cross. How did He dispense Himself into us? He gave His body and shed His blood for us. Shedding His blood was for redeeming us, and giving His body was for dispensing His life so that He could enter into us. Our remembrance of Him today is our reviewing once again how He shed His blood for us so that our sins would be forgiven, and how He gave His body on the cross so that we could gain Him. Now we have Him within us as our life. Our eating the bread and drinking the cup are to review and be reminded of the story of this salvation. We remember Him by eating, drinking, and enjoying Him.

At the same time, this kind of remembrance is the testimony of our daily lives. We testify that there is nothing in our daily lives but eating and drinking the Lord. Our daily lives are lives of enjoying the Lord, the Savior who gave His body and shed His blood for us. Moreover, we live out this One, testifying that for us to live is Christ. On the first day of the week, our coming together to break the bread unto the remembrance of the Lord is a declaration and a testimony in the universe that we belong to Christ. We have the Lord in us, and we enjoy Him every day. Every Lord's Day our coming together is to have a declaration, a remembrance, a display in the universe, and at the same time we remind ourselves that we love Him, we consider Him, and we are waiting for His coming back. This is the first significance of breaking the bread.

The second significance of bread-breaking is that we break the same bread and drink the same cup, implying that we have fellowship with one another. After being passed around, this one bread and one wine enter into each believer. One portion of the bread enters into me, and another portion enters into another. I take one drink of this cup, and another brother takes another drink. Each attendant partakes of the bread and the cup, taking the bread and wine into him. This proves that we are one and that we have fellowship with one another. We not only remember and enjoy the Lord, but through partaking of the bread and the cup we testify that we are one and that we are in one Body. In the oneness of the Body we have mutual fellowship and enjoyment together.

For this reason, before we remember the Lord and come together for this fellowship, we need to examine ourselves and ask for the Lord's shining. We need to confess our sins thoroughly, ask for the cleansing of the Lord's blood for our filthiness, and carefully deal with any hindrance before the Lord so that we have no barriers between us and Him or problems with one another. In this way we can sit at the Lord's table to eat Him, drink Him, enjoy Him, and have fellowship together.

Before we break bread in a home meeting, we need to lead the meeting gradually. We should not rush; we should make our practice lasting and stable. If a meeting for the breaking of bread cannot be established in three months, this is all right. We can wait until the fourth month, and if it still cannot be established, we can wait until the fifth month. We must always see how the Lord wants to lead the new ones and how they can follow the Lord to go on. If we wait until the situation is ready, we can establish the breaking of bread in one place after another. These are issues we should not ignore. We must never work too fast; rather, we should lead the new ones in life and help them in their living. From the beginning we should help them to have a serious attitude and pay attention to all these things so that they can take the right way and not damage their testimony in the future.

(A message given on March 3, 1987 in Taipei, Taiwan)

CHAPTER SIX

KEYS TO PERFECTING THE HOME MEETINGS

GIVING OURSELVES TO OTHERS

When we knock on doors, particularly to care for and perfect the home meetings, our greatest need is to give two things to others: first, ourselves and second, life and truth. In other words, it is to give ourselves and the Lord to others. The Lord is life and truth. The Lord Jesus came to earth not merely to do a work or merely to give some messages. He came to give Himself, to minister Himself, to man. To ordinary people today, their person is one matter and what they do is another. The Lord Jesus' work and ministry were not like this. The Lord Himself and His ministry cannot be separated. The Lord Himself was His ministry, and what He ministered was Himself. He gave Himself to man.

In Matthew 20, when the Lord's disciples were reasoning as to which of them was greatest, the Lord told them not to reason in that way; rather, they should learn to serve. "Just as the Son of Man did not come to be served, but to serve and to give His life as a ransom for many" (v. 28). The Lord gave His life for us. *Life* in the original Greek text means "soul," or "self," and refers to the complete person with a life and personality, including all that this person is. This "self" is the positive aspect of the person, not the negative self. God has His "self," His person. When the Lord Jesus was on earth, He too had His "self," His soul and person. You and I also have our self, which is our soul. The Lord laid down His life for us. This life was His self, His *psuche,* the soul life. Therefore, the first key to perfecting a home meeting is to give ourselves to others.

The Lord's Giving Himself to Us

The Lord said in John 10:11, "I am the good Shepherd; the good Shepherd lays down His life for the sheep." It is not that men forced Him to give His life but that He as the good Shepherd was willing to do it. He willingly laid down His life on the cross; He was willing to be "lifted up" on the cross (3:14). In the eyes of men it was the Jews who killed Him, while in the eyes of God it was God Himself who foreordained and arranged for Him to go to the cross. In the Lord Jesus' own eyes, however, it was neither merely the Jews nor God alone, but it was He Himself who willingly went to the cross to pour out His life for us. For the Lord to lay down His life means that He gave, bestowed, and granted His life. He gave Himself to us on the cross.

Examples of the Apostles' Giving Themselves in the New Testament

In the New Testament the apostle Paul also mentioned a number of times that he was willing to forsake his life for the saints. To forsake one's life is to give oneself to others. In 2 Corinthians 12:15 Paul said, "But I, I will most gladly spend and be utterly spent on behalf of your souls." Paul was willing to spend everything for the believers in Corinth. He was willing to spend even himself, to give himself, to the Corinthians.

In Acts 20:24 Paul also said, "But I consider my life of no account." *Life* here is the same word as in John 10:11, with the same meaning. Paul did not care for himself and had no regard for himself. He was for the ministry and commission of the Lord and was willing to give himself for that. The New Testament also mentions persons like Prisca and Aquila who risked their own necks (Rom. 16:3-4). According to the sense of the word in Greek, they risked their own lives, not caring about themselves. Paul's co-worker Epaphroditus was the same way (Phil 2:30). Again, *life* in these verses literally means "soul." To risk one's life is to risk one's person with his disposition, not caring about oneself and giving oneself to others. This is the pattern we should see and follow.

Giving Up Ourselves Being the Only Way to Perfect the Home Meetings

Being a person who serves the Lord full time, you have to let others feel that you truly give yourself entirely, not merely to do the work of door-knocking or merely to come to perfect home meetings, but to present yourself and to give yourself to them. Perhaps many people think that to forsake themselves is to become a martyr. To be sure, it is glorious if, as a result of receiving the Lord's leading, you are martyred for the Lord. However, if you are only martyred for the Lord, exerting yourself to the uttermost and not caring whether you live or die, what benefit will this bring to the new way? If we all go to be martyrs for the Lord, will the Lord be happy? Certainly not. If all are martyrs, there will be no one to do the work that needs to be done and bear the responsibilities that must be borne. To be martyred for the Lord without a proper and appropriate reason is to commit suicide in disguise. Many countries have their "suicide squads," yet for someone to risk his life inappropriately is to bring death upon himself. To do this has no meaning whatsoever.

When the Lord Jesus came to earth, He did not immediately give up His life to be martyred. Instead, He went step by step through the processes of life, being born, growing up, and so on. The Gospel of Luke shows us that His growing up was not ordinary but particular. He grew until He was thirty years of age, and during those thirty years He had many particular expressions. Philippians 2:7-8 says, "Becoming in the likeness of men; and being found in fashion as a man." This refers in part to His life as a carpenter in Nazareth before He began His ministry. He was found in fashion as a man. If we merely say that He was God becoming flesh, it is hard for people to understand what kind of flesh He was. However, through His thirty years of living on the earth He was seen as a man who was the same as everyone else. He slept, He ate, and He also wept. All His acts and deeds were those of a man. Therefore, men found Him in the likeness of men, and His life was full of meaning. When He reached thirty years of age, He began His ministry. His entire move was in His ministry, a genuine move of forsaking Himself.

At the beginning of John 7, the Jews were about to keep the Feast of Tabernacles. Jesus' brothers in the flesh said to Him, "Depart from here and go into Judea, so that Your disciples also may behold Your works which You are doing; for no one does anything in secret and himself seeks to be known openly" (vv. 3-4). What they meant was that since Jesus had such great abilities, He should hurry to Jerusalem to show them off. However, the Lord said to them, "My time has not yet come, but your time is always ready" (v. 6). This shows that even the Lord's crucifixion was according to a timetable; He knew that He could not arrive one day earlier. Thus, He told His disciples that He could not at that time go to die; the time had not come. Rather, He had to die at the exact time the Messiah should be cut off in order to fulfill the prophecy in the Old Testament.

Daniel 9:24-26 speaks of seventy weeks; after sixty-two weeks, Messiah would be cut off. That was the time when the Lord Jesus would be crucified on the cross. The Lord's crucifixion had a definite timetable. Those who know the Bible can calculate the time. According to history, from the decree for the rebuilding of Jerusalem to the time the Messiah would be cut off were first seven weeks and then sixty-two weeks, signifying four hundred eighty-three years. It was only when the four hundred eighty-third year had arrived that Christ could be crucified. The Lord Jesus Himself also knew that He needed to arrive at Jerusalem one day before the Passover because He is God's Passover Lamb and had to be killed on that day. Therefore, He did not risk His life to die merely as a martyr. He needed to preserve Himself for that day, which was the day of the Passover when He was to be killed, which was also the year the Messiah was to be cut off.

The Bible has a very clear account of this prophecy. Not only is the year and time recorded clearly, but even the place was also very clearly recorded. We all know that Abraham offered Isaac on Mount Moriah, which is the place where the Lord Jesus was crucified. Golgotha is Calvary, which is the peak of Moriah. In the Old Testament Abraham offered his son Isaac on Mount Moriah, but God prepared a ram at that time to be Isaac's substitute (Gen. 22:13). The ram is a type of

Christ. This is a clear evidence of the place in which the Lord was to die. If the Lord Jesus were crucified in Galilee, that would be wrong; if He were crucified in Bethlehem, that also would be incorrect. Even to be crucified in Jerusalem would be wrong. The Lord must be crucified outside the city on Calvary, the peak of Mount Moriah, so that He could fulfill the prophecy in the Old Testament.

When the Lord Jesus was on the earth, He was crucified not merely at the time of His crucifixion. Rather, He began to live the life of crucifixion as soon as He commenced His ministry. He laid down His life daily. In other words, the Lord Jesus gave His life for us not only for a few hours on the cross; He began to give His life from the commencement of His ministry. He lived a life of laying down His life and did a work of forsaking His life. His entire living and work was to give His life. He gave Himself up and gave Himself entirely to us. Today we who go out to knock on doors also need to forsake ourselves as the Lord did. If we do not deny ourselves, we cannot knock on doors. Common people would prefer to sit on the couch at home, watch television, and rest when they are tired. This is a very carefree life. However, when we knock on doors, we need to see people face to face, and when we talk to them, we must observe their expressions. This requires us to deny ourselves.

When the Lord Jesus began His ministry, He also observed people's expressions. Sometimes when people were not right or did not welcome Him, He would not work there but would go away. Often when something was not right, He turned away, acting not according to men's will but according to God's will. Although He was the sovereign One, sometimes He performed miracles, but sometimes He did not. No matter how people urged Him, He did not move right away. When people were hurried or anxious, He was not, but if He truly wanted to perform a miracle, no one could stop Him. When He calmed the wind and the sea, He only needed to rebuke them once; the wind stopped immediately, and the waves died down. In the Gospels we see Peter complaining to Him, "Teacher, does it not matter to You that we are perishing?" (Mark 4:38). Peter seemed to be saying to the Lord, "We follow You, yet we

have come to an end here. We are perishing, but You are not
taking care of us." Very often in our experience of the Lord we
think that we are perishing and that the Lord does not take
care of us. We should know this: If the Lord does not seem to
take care of us, we must then have the experience of forsaking
ourselves. For example, when we go out door-knocking, we
often like to pray, "O Lord, let us see nice faces. Let us meet
sons of peace." However, wonderfully, the Lord sometimes
does not give us a son of peace for the whole day. When we
knock on one door, out comes a "wolf." When we knock on
another one, the "wolf" howls at us, and when we knock on a
third door, the "wolf" wants to eat us. At this juncture if we
are not willing to deny ourselves, we will give up. However, if
we begin to lay ourselves down, to deny ourselves, we will continue to knock on doors.

Men are changeable. We should never completely believe in
their condition. They are like the weather in certain places
which always changes. However, a man's face changes quicker
than the weather. It may be that today when we knock on doors,
we will come across cold and unfriendly faces. If we knock on
the same door again the day after tomorrow, the faces may
look even worse, and if we knock on the door yet another
day, the person there may use abusive language against us.
However, if we can deny ourselves and continue with our door-
knocking, on the fifth or sixth time the same one who spoke
abusively will become a son of peace. Therefore, as we knock
on doors, it is difficult to determine when a person will be
saved. In our own experience, not all of us were sons of peace
at first. We also may have looked cold and unfriendly to the
persons who visited us. Eventually though, we were all saved
and have become sons of peace. If we are willing to deny ourselves and knock on doors unceasingly and steadfastly, many
"sons of Gehenna" will become "sons of peace."

Denying Ourselves Being
to Come out of Our Own Disposition

The four Gospels give a clear account of the Lord Jesus'
walk. When the Lord Jesus was on the earth, He denied Himself in all aspects and at all times. Therefore, when we go to

perfect home meetings, we must be ones who deny ourselves. To deny ourselves is to not preserve ourselves. For example, some brothers have a natural disposition of seldom opening their mouths. No matter what other people say, they keep their mouths shut. Although for many years in the church we have been taught that our being must be broken and that our self, whether good or bad, must be dealt with, this teaching is still useless to brothers like this. They are not willing to deny themselves and open their mouths. If brothers of this kind go to perfect home meetings, they will definitely have no success because they have not come out of themselves. They have not come out of their disposition.

Disposition is the negative aspect of our self, a self that is not good. There may be no particular matter that is wrong in this kind of self, but when everyone else is burning in spirit, a person with a quiet disposition is "fireproof," even "fire extinguishing." If this kind of person goes to visit or perfect home meetings, there will be no impact, because he has not denied himself. Therefore, if we wish to go to someone's house and perfect the home meeting there, we first need to be persons who deny ourselves. We need to lay down our disposition and blend with others. In this way, we are no longer the same as we were. Rather, we have changed. To be changed means that we have denied ourselves. A quiet person thinks that silence is very good, but if he always remains silent, he has not denied himself. That silence will kill people. Others have a lively and active disposition. The more lively and active such a one is, the more he kills others. Only if he calms down can anyone else survive and stay living. In the Bible to forsake the self also means to deny oneself, to go against oneself. This is what we refer to when we speak of bearing an anti-testimony. This anti-testimony is a testimony of going against oneself. If we go out every day, bearing an anti-testimony and going against our disposition, we will succeed.

Giving Ourselves to Others Meaning to Be Changed

In fact, giving ourselves to others means that we are changed. When we go to perfect home meetings, we must be changed. Those who prefer laughing need to learn how to weep, while those who prefer weeping need to learn how to laugh. Those who do not speak need to keep speaking; those who speak too much must begin to keep silent. This is giving one-self to others. For example, some brothers pray very fervently and freely in the meetings. However, when we go to perfect home meetings, we should never do this. If we are too fervent and released, we will frighten people away. We must learn to observe the situation and follow the Holy Spirit. We should not allow ourselves to speak, call a hymn, sing, or proclaim casually.

The first person in the New Testament who went against Himself was the Lord Jesus. We see from the Gospels that when people were burning, the Lord was very calm, and when people were silent, He rose up to take action. This often disturbed the disciples, because they did not understand. In John 11:1-16, when Lazarus was sick and about to die, his sisters Martha and Mary sent people to beg the Lord Jesus to come to them quickly. Perhaps the disciples also urged Him, asking Him to go quickly to heal Lazarus. However, the Lord Jesus did not move. This must have puzzled the disciples. The Lord Jesus had always loved Martha, Mary, and Lazarus. He also had performed many miracles and healed many people on His way. However, when His friend was sick, He appeared indifferent. Why was this? He first remained in the place where He was for two days and then told the disciples that He wanted to go and see Lazarus. This puzzled the disciples even more. If He had wanted to go, why had He not gone earlier? At that time there may have been a chance for Lazarus to live. Now that Lazarus had died, what was the purpose of going? Furthermore, the Lord Jesus was far away across the Jordan, but Lazarus lived in Judea near Jerusalem, where the Jews were planning to kill Him. Yet the Lord Jesus did not care; He insisted on going to see Lazarus. Although the disciples had an opposite opinion, they could only accompany Him and plan to die with Him. In the Gospels the Lord Jesus was often like this, going against Himself.

Going against Ourselves to Perfect Others

When we go to perfect the home meetings, we need to be

persons who counter ourselves. Once we counter ourselves, our spirit will come out, the Lord will come out, and we will have the way. Throughout our living we pray often. When we pray, we frequently have the experience that the feeling within is leading us to counter ourselves, that is, to hate ourselves. However, not more than five minutes after our prayer our old way and old self come out again, and we remain the same. Then when the time comes to go to perfect the home meetings, we still rely on ourselves. Therefore, we need to guard our praying spirit all the time, the spirit that goes against ourselves. For example, we may not feel happy for the whole day, but we may still need to go to perfect a home meeting in the evening. If we do not counter our self, we will be an unhappy person going to perfect the home meeting. How can such an unhappy person perfect a home meeting? In order to perfect a home meeting, we must counter our self, at least our unhappy self, to become a person who rejoices in the Lord. In this way we can perfect the home meeting.

Some people often ask why their work has no effect. Their work has no effect because they are too much in themselves. When they give messages, they are in themselves, and when they speak with others, they are in themselves. Eventually, the Lord cannot do anything. We need to counter our self. It is only by countering our self that we can give ourselves to others as a clean person. Once we counter ourselves, we become clean. If we do not counter ourselves, our whole being is full of germs. As a result, although we have given ourselves to others, what we have given is a filthy, old man. If we have read the four Gospels carefully, we will see that when the Lord Jesus worked, He went against Himself. Those who have read the Acts and the Epistles will also see that many saints, especially Paul, were also such persons. Once they began working, they all countered themselves. Therefore, they could deny themselves and become the supply for others, and their work was able to have a genuine impact.

More than fifty years ago there was an evangelist, John Sung, who was very powerful in gospel preaching. In 1933 he went to my hometown to preach the gospel. During one meeting we were all sitting there waiting for the meeting to begin.

Suddenly he came in singing, "Down with sin, down with sin; out with the devil, out with the devil." At that time, as the national army was moving north to fight against the foreign nations and warlords, the army was singing, "Down with foreigners, down with foreigners; out with warlords, out with warlords." John Sung adopted the tune of that song, changed the lyrics, and began to sing them as he entered the meeting. As soon as he entered the meeting singing, others followed his singing. Eventually, everyone was singing freely and everyone was released. By the time he went to the podium to deliver his message, it was very easy for him to speak. When we go to perfect home meetings, we need to start singing hymns while we are still at home and bring a joyful spirit to the meeting to continue the singing there. In this way, in the homes that we visit the whole family will surely become vital and functioning. This is what is meant by giving ourselves to others.

We all have had this kind of experience. Our natural person does not like to read the Bible and fellowship with the Lord. However, we are now persons who counter ourselves. Not only do we like to fellowship with the Lord, but we also are willing to read the Bible, pray, sing hymns, give praises, and release our spirit. This is because the Lord is within us and makes us willing to counter ourselves. If we all counter ourselves in this way, we will be able to perfect any home we visit. The kind of persons we are determines the persons whom we can perfect. Time and again we can go to visit the homes and perfect the ones there. Eventually, they will spontaneously speak what we speak and do what we do. This is the perfecting of the home meetings.

GIVING LIFE AND TRUTH TO OTHERS

Each time we go to a home meeting, we must have the definite goal of supplying truth and life to others. On the one hand, we need to encourage the new ones to ask questions in the home meetings, while on the other hand, we should not expect to deal too much with their problems. This is not to say that we will not solve their problems but that we should not intend to solve their problems. We should know that the One who can truly benefit others is the Lord Himself. Where is the

Lord? The Lord, in one aspect, is in His life and in another aspect, He is in His truth. Every time we go to perfect a home meeting, we must have a definite goal: to give a particular spiritual truth to others and to supply life to them. However, while we are working, we cannot refuse to accommodate them, but neither should we be too accommodating. If we do not accommodate them, we will kill them, but if we do accommodate them, there must be a limit to how much we are prepared to do. We have to adhere to this limit and stay within it. Then we can supply life and truth to them in a definite way.

We may use as an example our current burden to help the new ones understand the breaking of bread and to help them become ones who love the Lord, desire Him, and seek Him. Our goal is to help them in such a way that they will have a turning point in life. We want them to see that we break the bread not because we have been admitted into a religion or that we follow a religious ceremony, but that breaking the bread will help them to have a turning point in their life and become ones who love the Lord and desire Him. For the first twenty-five minutes of a forty-minute meeting, the new ones may still be asking various kinds of questions. This is all right, because they are still spiritual children, but we ourselves need to hold firm to our goal and the timing of the meeting. In the remaining fifteen minutes, we need to give them a "shot" to inject them with the burden that we have brought with us. It is probably the case that by this time we have not resolved their problems and have not finished answering their questions, but those matters are secondary. The purpose of our visit is not to answer questions or solve their problems but to inject the truth concerning the breaking of bread into them. In this way, they can gain help regarding the breaking of bread, receive light from the truth, and receive the life supply. If we work in this way every week for the fifty-two weeks in a year, in the long run much life supply and enlightenment of the truth will be wrought into them. In not more than a year we will see that they have had a turn in life, growth in truth, and more knowledge of the Lord and the spiritual matters.

When we perfect the home meetings, we need to have a

burden and a long-term view. Otherwise, we are merely carrying out a meeting, which is not very meaningful. We can compare our work to that of a teacher. We need to teach our "students" definite items in each lesson and not be ambivalent, considering that it does not matter what we do. If a teacher does not teach well, the students will have no improvement in the long run.

Because among us the truth is rich and the supply of life is readily available, we do not lack the proper materials. Thus, we should all the more go to perfect the home meetings step by step, the same way we take care of our own children, carefully considering what food to give them each day, whether meat, fish, vegetables, or perhaps all three. All the foregoing items need our consideration.

GIVING OUR PUBLICATIONS TO THE ONES WE CONTACT

Whenever we participate in a home meeting, we need to bring our publications with us. Since we now have fifteen thousand people who are newly baptized, there may not be enough manpower to take care of each family. Therefore, we should put out a small publication once every month and send it to the new ones. Through this publication we will be able to maintain our contact with them. In it there will be some correspondence, some life supply, some unveiling of the truth, a word concerning the gospel, and so on. We can also use this publication to announce certain activities of the church. I believe this will be a great help to them. However, this requires many prayers from all of us.

Since many of the newly baptized ones are educated people, they like to read something during their leisure. If we can give them some publications to keep in their homes, they will benefit from whatever they read, regardless of which item or page they turn to. The members of their family who read it will also gain the benefit. In this world today we need to rely on teaching through literature in whatever we do. The medium of literature is a truly powerful force. We need to use it wisely for our practical needs.

(A message given on March 5, 1987 in Taipei, Taiwan)

CHAPTER SEVEN

LEADING PEOPLE TO KNOW THE CHURCH

THE MEETINGS IN THE NEW WAY

The New Testament reveals to us that the Lord's universal church is manifested locality by locality, and in every locality the church's meetings are mostly in the homes of the saints. Hence, the home is the basic unit of the church life. Undoubtedly, the church's meetings include big meetings and medium-sized meetings, but the basic meeting place is the home. The basic pattern for meeting is the meeting in the homes. Acts 12 mentions that while Peter was in prison, the church was praying for him fervently. After Peter came out from the prison, he went to the house of Mary, a sister, the mother of John, where there was a considerable number of people assembled together and praying (vv. 5, 12). Here we see the prayer of the church carried out by the assembling of the saints in a home. This record does not tell us that the church held a big meeting to pray for Peter. Rather, it says that it was in a house that a considerable number of people assembled together to pray. We believe that this home was only one of many that was very close to Peter, a home that cared for Peter very much.

It is hard to determine at what time Peter arrived at that house, but it is likely that it was late at night (v. 6). This shows us that the church meeting at that time was not similar to today's religious worship, which is almost always in the same place on definite dates and at set times. Of course, having definite dates and set times is more convenient for the sake of scheduling our daily living and activities. However, the Bible shows us that the church meetings are not regulated and rigidly organized. Rather, they are meant to meet the needs. Whenever there is a need, there is a meeting, and the meeting can be in any of the homes.

The revelation of the Bible is that the meetings of the church are not religious; rather, they are the activity of the Body. The church is the Body of Christ. If the activity of a body is too regulated and organized, the body will seem more like a puppet or a robot. Although the regulations of our training are rather strict, we should exercise some liberty. If we are too regulated, we may easily become like puppets. The church meetings are not basically in the big meetings or in the meeting halls but in the homes of the saints. This requires us to be spiritual, to have the divine life and the work of the Holy Spirit, to be transformed in life, and to be filled with the Holy Spirit.

As we all know, the purpose of any religion is to have an object of worship and to teach according to that object. Due to man's desire to worship God, he feels the need for a place of gathering in which one man speaks and all the others listen. As a result, a religion is produced. However, religion does not require spirituality or the divine life, and neither does it require transformation in life or the filling of the Holy Spirit. Instead, it requires only man's presence. There is no need of training, growth, or learning. It is sufficient that people merely attend the meetings. For a person to come every time is an honor to the meeting, and for him to make a material offering is excellent. This is religion. Today's Christianity, including Catholicism, Protestantism, every sect, and every denomination, is in such a condition. They establish seminaries to train theological students to preach. Then these become assistant pastors, then pastors, and finally hold higher offices. The clergy perform their duties and manage the things regarding the worship of God. The remaining ones are all laymen. They need neither to learn the things concerning worship nor to do much during the meetings.

We may use planting flowers as an example. For a flower to grow properly, much effort and even special care are required. After the seed is sown, there must be no lack of water, fertilizer, weeding, or pesticides. If the flower is soaked with too much water, it will die, but if it is watered too little, it will wither. Often, attention should be given even to the amount of oxygen required by the flower. If the flower is always kept inside the house, its leaves will turn yellow; then it will need to be placed outside. All these matters require much time and energy. Therefore, some people simply buy artificial flowers. Then there is no need to worry about insects, watering, and the condition of the air. By spending a little money, people can enjoy their flowers without any labor. To speak a frank word, today's Christianity is mostly doing the work of "artificial flowers." We are laboring here in an earnest way while certain ones are laughing behind our backs and saying that we are bringing trouble on ourselves. It is true that we are laboring and have troubles. All our labor is to produce not artificial flowers but the real items.

As people in the world all know, to do something well involves many difficulties. We may illustrate this by the difference between a doll and a real child. To buy a doll and keep it at home is very easy. Today many dolls are made to look like real children; some not only can walk but can also sing. With only a doll at home, we do not need to cook and to feed it, and we never need to change its diapers. This saves us much effort. However, when a real baby is born, many troubles come. Then we need to change diapers, bathe him, and feed him, and if he gets sick, we need to find a doctor for him. Parents all know that to raise a child truly is not easy. It is inexcusable to give birth to a child but not raise him. Parents will regret very much if they are unable to keep their child alive. We have taken the new way to gain many new ones, but if we cannot raise every one properly, we will owe something to the Lord, and we will also lose our credibility. Hence, we must feed these new ones so that they become healthy and functioning members. This is our burden.

The Lord said that He will come quickly (Rev. 22:20). From the time He spoke this until now, two thousand years have passed, but He still has not come. What has delayed Him? It is the condition of the church. If we study the history of the church and the situation of today's Christianity, we will groan deeply because the Lord has not gained what He wants. If we look at Catholicism carefully and go to their masses, we will understand the real situation there, and if we go to the Vatican, we will understand the Bible's prophecies in Revelation, which say that one day the Lord will burn up all those things. The Lord truly has gained nothing in all of that. We have also observed the situation in Protestantism, at least in the Far East. Even though Protestantism preached the gospel and taught the truth, the Lord was able to gain very little from that in actuality.

The Lord prophesied that when He comes again, He will come as a thief (3:3; 16:15). As we all know, a thief comes to steal not the refuse but the treasure. If the Lord comes today, where can He find a treasure to steal? He can find it almost nowhere. It is not necessary to speak of the outward situation in religion; even among us in the Lord's recovery there is not much treasure. For years, we have been struggling, fighting the influence of Christianity. The background, environment, and situation of Christianity today have too great an influence. Some who came from New Zealand and Australia told us that they were deeply oppressed there and restricted by Christianity's background and environment, which was very hard for them to overcome. Here in Taiwan it is the same. This causes the Lord's work to be very limited. This is the reason why we need to change our system.

Those who have been to the United States know that flying from Taiwan to Los Angeles takes only eleven hours, but flying from Los Angeles back to Taiwan takes thirteen hours. There is a two hour difference due to the direction of the wind. When going along with the wind, the arrival time is two hours earlier. When going against the wind, arrival is two hours later. The situation in today's Christianity is the same; it is almost always "against the wind." Today we are taking the new way of knocking on doors to lead people to be saved. This is a hard job, but we have succeeded. However, following this we need to perfect the home meetings, which is an even harder job. Therefore, the burden on us is truly heavy, and our feeling is even heavier. I hope we will all rise up to bear the burden together to perfect the home meetings.

THE NEED OF THE NEW ONES—TO KNOW THE CHURCH

When we go out to perfect the home meetings, we need to be aware of the needs of the new ones. This can be compared to a mother raising children. She needs to know when to change their diapers and when to nurse them. Generally speaking, all these things have a set time, but in reality children also have urgent needs that must be taken care of. Similarly, in the matter of perfecting the home meetings, we also need to take care of the urgent needs. At present we are facing an urgent need. Sooner or later the newly saved ones will all ask, "We have been baptized, but where is the church? Where do we go to meet?"

According to the principle, we have not wanted these newly baptized ones to come to our existing meetings right away. Once they come to our existing meetings, they may see our old religious condition and be affected. Since we do not want them to be infected, we have preferred to slow down, not mentioning the church too soon and not letting them know about the church too quickly. Nevertheless, this is like teaching a mother how to raise her children, telling her when to change diapers and when not to change them. If a new mother, who has never raised any children before and has had no experience, receives this teaching, her child may suffer. When his diaper is wet, she will not change it because she is strictly following the teaching to not change diapers until the prescribed time. This causes many problems. At this time many newly baptized brothers and sisters have a need—they want to know the church—but due to our keeping the old fellowship, no one will answer their questions.

In our application, we must learn how to be flexible. When a child's diaper is wet, we should still change it, even if it does not seem to be the right time. If we continue to wait, problems will arise. Thus, if people ask where our church is, we should tell them honestly where our meeting hall is located. Usually good doctors do not have too many regulations in their treatment. Doctors who strictly follow rules and regulations are novices; experienced doctors usually adapt to the circumstances with boldness and attentiveness. Thirty years ago, a certain brother among us was a good, flexible doctor. On the one hand, he absolutely had the view of Western medicine; on the other hand, he also fully understood the effectiveness of Chinese medicine in healing sickness. Therefore, many people received his help. We should be like him, not being rigid. Rigidity kills people. Only adaptability, flexibility, and pliability can render genuine help to people.

At this time, we need to lead the new ones to know the church. The church is a great topic in the New Testament. The Old Testament does not expressly and clearly speak about the church, but it does have many types and prophecies concerning the church. It is in the New Testament, in Matthew 16:18, that the Lord Jesus used the word *church* for the first time. This is the first mention of the church in the Bible. Therefore, this is a revelation and very important truth in the New Testament.

In 1957 we invited a famous preacher from abroad to speak to us in Taipei. This gave rise to a problem regarding the ground of the church. After that we released thirty-six messages concerning the ground of the church and published them in a book called *The Testimony and the Ground of the Church*. This is a very great topic, and we should not take it lightly. However, when we go out to preach, we must speak in a way that is easy to understand, just as a mother becomes a "good doctor" who makes important nutrients and medicines into something very convenient and easy to take in. As far as we know, there are already one hundred fifty homes among us beginning to have the Lord's table meeting. In principle, once we begin to have the Lord's table meetings, we should speak to the saints concerning the church, letting the ones who break the bread know what the church is. The breaking of bread, the church, and the Body of Christ are different aspects of one thing. Therefore, since we break bread in the homes, we need to mention the church.

In meeting the needs, we need to be adaptable and flexible, just as a coach teaches people how to play basketball. Having learned the basic techniques of carrying, passing, and shooting the ball, the players still need to be adaptable when they play on the court. I hope that when we go to perfect the home meetings, we will definitely put this into practice. On the other hand, we must not be too rigid in following regulations because this will kill people. Following rules too closely kills people, but transgressing them too much also damages them. We must turn back to our spirit and follow our spirit. This basic fellowship is to help us to apply what we have in the home meetings.

WHAT THE CHURCH IS

A Called-out Congregation

When we speak about the church to the new ones, we first need to help them to understand what the church is. In Chinese culture and history there was never such a thing as the church. Because of this, there is no such term even in the bigger Chinese lexicons and dictionaries.

What is the church? Simply speaking, the church is first of all the called-out congregation, or assembly. The Greek word for *church, ekklesia,* is composed of two words, *ek* and *klesia. Ek* has the meaning of "out," while *klesia* refers to a calling. Together these two words mean "a called-out congregation." When the leaders of ancient Greek cities wanted to gather together all the people in the city, they would call them out. This assembly was the *ekklesia,* the called-out congregation.

In the New Testament when the Lord Jesus came out for His ministry and spoke of the church (Matt. 16:18), He used this term—*ekklesia,* a called-out congregation. The Lord Jesus' use of this term was proper and very significant. Two to three centuries ago, Christianity was spread to China. When the people in Christianity wanted to translate this term, they were influenced by Catholicism and Protestantism in a religious way, thinking that *ekklesia* was a religious gathering. Therefore, they translated it into *chiao-hui,* "religious gathering." While *hui* (gathering) was correctly translated, *chiao* (religious) was a misinterpretation. The English usage of the word *church* may also be inaccurate, because most people consider the church as a chapel. Beginning from 1829 when the Brethren were raised up, including J. N. Darby, they carefully studied this word and learned that *ekklesia* refers to a called-out congregation. After that they no longer used the word *church;* rather, they changed it to *assembly.* Though the word *assembly* is very good, its meaning in the English language is not as rich as that in the Greek language.

The Open Brethren arrived in China very early, but they did not correct the use of *chiao* (religious) in *chiao-hui* (religious congregation) and continued to follow the usage of Christianity. Then in 1915 the Assemblies of God were raised up in the United States. They followed the Brethren in using the word *assembly* in their name. After that, around 1930, they came to China. When they landed in China, they immediately translated the word *assembly* into *chao-hui* (assembly). This translation was good and accurate.

At this time while we are translating the New Testament, we hope to eliminate all religious concepts as much as possible and translate according to the Greek language. Hence, we have translated *chiao-hui* (religious gathering) into *chao-hui* (assembly). We hope that gradually in our utterance and nomenclature we will change from *chiao-hui* into *chao-hui.* While *chao-hui* is scriptural, *chiao-hui* has a religious color. The church is the called-out congregation of God. God has given Christ to be Head over all things to the church (Eph. 1:22).

The Body of Christ

Second, Ephesians 1:23 tells us that the church is the Body of Christ. Some Bible expositors have said that *Body* is a metaphor, an illustration. This is incorrect. The Body in Ephesians is a fact. The church is a Body, the Body of Christ. The Body may appear to be an organization, but in actuality it is not. A table assembled together from twenty interlaced pieces of wood is an organization. A mere pile of wood, however, is not considered an organization. It is only when we organize this pile of wood piece by piece that it is an organization, such as a table or a bookshelf. Our body may look like an organization, but it is not; it is an organism. An organization does not have life and activity, but our body has both life and activity. If life ceases, all our members can no longer move. When life is gone, there is no activity. The church is not an organization. The church is an organism in the divine life of God. It is joined and knit together as an organism.

Ephesians 1:22-23 says, "The church,...the fullness of the One who fills all in all." This Christ is the One who fills all in all, and the church is His fullness. We may illustrate fullness with a cup of water. There may be water in a cup, but people cannot see it. If the cup is not full, the water is hidden in it. When the cup is filled with water to its limit and the water overflows, there is the fullness of the water, which is also the expression of the water. Now what is in the cup can be clearly seen by all. Similarly, the church is the overflow of Christ, and the overflowing of Christ is the fullness.

Fullness is the expression of the overflow of the riches. Fullness is not something an organization can express. Rather, fullness is a condition of life. When life grows to a certain extent, there is an expression. We may illustrate this with a newborn babe. A newborn is small, short, and very thin; this is its expression. However, when he grows unto the fullness of life, he is expressed in his tallness and strength. This is the expression of his fullness. The Chinese express the riches of China, while the Americans express the riches of America. When many American brothers were young, they were small and thin, but now they have all become very big, being filled with American eggs, chicken, steak, oranges, and so forth. All this food passed through them in digestion, producing organic changes and becoming their constitution. Now they are the aggregate of all these riches, and this aggregate is the expression of the riches of America. The more we eat Christ and enjoy Christ, the more we become His overflow and expression. This is the church.

If we have this light and see the church according to this light, we will realize that the church cannot be found in Christianity. The church is not merely the accumulation of all the baptized ones. This is an organization, a gathering, but not the church, the Body of Christ. Today in the Lord's recovery we do not want an organization or merely a gathering. Instead, we need an organism. For this reason, we are hoping to change the big meetings, because it is easy for the big meetings merely to be a gathering, an organization, which lacks the element of life. We want to have many small home meetings to allow life to grow from within. This is not a matter of work but of growth. As life grows, it produces a condition—the fullness of Christ to express Christ. This is the called-out assembly of God, the church.

The House of God

Third, the church is the house of God. We should not understand the meaning of *house* completely according to our human concept. *House* can refer both to a dwelling place and a family. The family is a house, and the dwelling place is also a house. In the Greek language these are the same word with the same meaning. The house of God is the dwelling place of God, His family, and also the members of His household. The church is not only the house of God, but also the household of God. The church is this group of family members as a household.

What is the function of this household, this house? Paul said that the church is the pillar and base of the truth (1 Tim. 3:15b). This word is based on the architecture of the eastern coast of the Mediterranean, the land of Judah and of ancient Greece. Jewish and ancient Greek constructions began with a base, pillars were built on top of it, and then the rest of the building continued upward. Therefore, the entire construction was supported by the pillars on this base. This is what it means to be the pillar and the base. To God, the church has this kind of function to bear all that God is as the reality, the truth, of the universe. The word *reality* is better than *truth* in conveying the proper meaning, because *truth* can be misunderstood as doctrines. This may cause people to think that the church holds doctrines. No, the church is not for holding doctrines but for holding the reality of all that God is. In the universe, only God is reality; all that He is is reality, which is borne by the church. We are here as the church, the house and household of God, holding the reality of all that God is.

God Manifested in the Flesh

First Timothy 3:16 says, "Great is the mystery of godliness: He who was manifested in the flesh." This word refers not only to Christ but also to all the elements in the church. In other words, not only is Christ the great mystery of godliness, but in principle the church is the same; the church is God manifested in the flesh. When the Lord Jesus was on the earth, God was manifested in His flesh. Today God is also manifested in the flesh in the church on the earth. We can prove this from the sequence in these verses. The end of this portion says, "Preached among the nations, / Believed on in the world, / Taken up in glory." If this mystery refers only to Christ, then Christ's being taken up in glory should precede His being preached among the nations. Here, however, being taken up in glory is after being believed on in the world. This proves that the great mystery of godliness includes the church.

This gives us a comprehensive understanding and knowledge concerning the church. In application, however, we need to lead the new ones item by item according to their condition. We have to let them know that the church is the called-out assembly of God; the church is the Body of Christ, the fullness of Christ as His expression; the church is the house of God, which holds all that God is as the reality; and at the same time the church is the manifestation of God in the flesh. Perhaps they cannot fully understand all this, but after a while they will know it spontaneously. This is similar to learning mathematics. In the beginning we learn addition, finding it very easy. Then we learn subtraction, feeling that is a bit more difficult. After that we learn multiplication and division, and we may find memorizing the multiplication table to be even harder. At the time we are learning all these things, we do not thoroughly understand them, but through more learning, we gradually come to understand. Our leading the new ones is in the same principle. At the beginning they may not understand, but gradually they will. We simply should sow the seeds into their being and teach them. One day these seeds will blossom and bear fruit.

THE TWO ASPECTS OF THE CHURCH

The Universal Aspect

The church has two aspects: the universal aspect and the

local aspect. As far as the universal aspect is concerned, the church is as big as the universe. Ephesians 1:23 says that Christ is the One who fills all in all. Since the church is His fullness, certainly it is also universal. In Matthew 16:18 the Lord Jesus speaks of the church, referring to its universal aspect; the Lord will build His church on "this rock," the revelation Peter received concerning Christ as the Son of the living God. Since the Lord is building the church upon this revelation, the church is certainly universal. Modern physicists such as Einstein define the universe as all space and time. The Chinese refer to the whole universe as "ancient and modern, Chinese and foreign." In the church, which encompasses "ancient and modern, Chinese and foreign," Paul was ancient, and you and I are modern; Paul was foreign, while you and I are Chinese. This is the universal church. The universal church has a progression of two thousand years. Regardless of time and space, all those who have believed in the Lord—from ancient to modern, from Chinese to foreign—added together are the universal church. This is the church in its universal aspect.

The Local Aspect

The church in another aspect is local. The local aspect is very easy to see. When we are in Taipei, we are the church in Taipei; this is local. Simultaneously, there are the church in Kaohsiung and the church in Hong Kong. This is the local aspect. The Lord Jesus said in Matthew 18:15-17 that if a brother sins against you and he does not listen to two or three witnesses, you should tell this to the church. This certainly does not refer to the universal church, the church that encompasses ancient and modern, Chinese and foreign. Rather, it refers to the church that is in your locality. If a brother sins against you, it would be very troublesome to tell it to the universal church, because it is difficult to find the universal church. But praise the Lord, there is an expression of the universal church right in your locality! This expression is the church in your locality. If you are in Taichung, you can go to the church in Taichung conveniently. Today many countries have established district courts for deciding local affairs.

Similarly, the universal church is expressed in the local churches. This is the local aspect of the church.

THE DESIGNATION OF THE CHURCH

Not Having a Special Name

In referring to the church, we speak of a designation but not a name, because the church in fact has no name. For example, the moon does not have a name; the moon has only a designation, which is "the moon." At most, we may say that the moon in Taipei is rounder than the moon in Kaohsiung, or the moon in the United States is bigger than the moon in Taiwan. In reality, though, it is the same moon. The one seen in the United States is the moon in the United States, and the one seen in Taiwan is the moon in Taiwan. Apart from this, the moon is unique and does not have any special name. It is the same with the church. Sadly, the various denominations in Christianity all have their special, unique names, such as the Baptists, the Presbyterians, the Methodists, the Anglicans, the Lutherans, and the Evangelical Lutherans. Once there is a difference, there is a separation, and once there is a separation, there is a sect. For this reason, we realize that we cannot hold on to any names. The church is uniquely one in the universe without any special name.

Using the Name of the Locality

The Bible shows us that since the church is expressed in a locality, we can use the locality as a designation. For example, the church located in Taipei is the church in Taipei. The one situated in Hong Kong is the church in Hong Kong, and the one positioned in London is the church in London. To designate a church after its locality is for people in the world to know where the church is. This is clearly indicated in Revelation 1:11. In the New Testament there are many of these designations. For example, in Acts 8:1 there is the church in Jerusalem, and in Romans 16:1 there is the church in Cenchrea. There are also the church in Colossae, the church in Ephesus, the church in Smyrna, and so on. All of these are the one church in each locality.

QUESTION AND ANSWER

Question: Since the church can have a designation, when the meeting hall needs to put up a sign, how should we designate it? This is a testimony to let the newly baptized ones know which church they belong to.

Answer: Due to administrative government regulations, every meeting hall requires a registration. Churches also require registration, so for this purpose we need a name. Therefore, we use "Assembly Hall" as our name to register with the government. For example, the church in Taipei is registered as the "Juridical Party of Taiwan, the church in Taipei Assembly Hall." This is due to the requirement of the law, society, and administrative procedures.

If the newly saved ones ask questions concerning the church, we need to give them a proper answer, telling them what the church is and the two aspects of the church. At the same time, we need to tell them that in Taipei there is only one church, and since the church in Taipei has so many people, it is subdivided into different district meetings. There are meetings in the hall, meetings in the districts, and also meetings in the homes. We can go to home meetings during the week, district meetings on the Lord's Day, and if we are willing, we can also go to the meetings in the meeting hall. In this way, we will answer the questions in their heart.

(A message given on March 10, 1987 in Taipei, Taiwan)

CHAPTER EIGHT

LEADING PEOPLE TO KNOW THE TRUTH CONCERNING SECTS

When the new way reaches a critical point, it will come to a peak, which is the home meetings. The way to lead the home meetings, perfect the home meetings, and go on in the home meetings is altogether critical to the success of the new way. Going door-knocking, visiting people, leading people to believe in the Lord and be saved, and baptizing them are only the basic matters. After a person is saved, establishing a meeting in his home, leading people in the meeting, and perfecting the meeting are the key matters. For us to climb this high peak is not easy at all. All of us, older ones and younger ones, need to understand this burden, receive this burden, and bear this burden in one accord.

THE TWO BASIC ELEMENTS OF A CHRISTIAN MEETING— THE SPIRIT AND THE WORD

There is a definite principle that the Spirit and the Word are needed for leading and perfecting a meeting. The Spirit and the Word are the two fundamental elements of Christian meetings. The Spirit is the Holy Spirit and the Word is the Bible. For us to be filled with the Spirit, we need to seek the Lord every day, pray unceasingly, be dealt with before the Lord, and be emptied and open to the Lord completely. In so doing, we can be filled with the Spirit every day. Therefore, to be filled with the Spirit simply requires our seeking, which is not too difficult.

To deal with the Word is not as simple. The Word is the Bible, which has existed among Christians for almost two thousand years. During the Dark Ages, the Bible was locked up by Catholicism for almost ten centuries. It was not until the early 1500s that the Reformation under Luther began to open the lock to release the Bible from the imprisonment of Catholicism. Along with the Reformation, the invention of printing and the use of newspapers brought a noticeable benefit for Christianity. The Bible began to be printed for public distribution, later spreading to every kind of Christian meeting. Today almost all Christians have a Bible in their hands. Unfortunately, although this Bible was unlocked and released, its intrinsic revelation and the profound meaning of its contents still remained unopened.

In the 1800s, three hundred years after the Reformation at the time of Luther, the Lord raised up the Brethren in England. They were very blessed before God and were full of light and revelation. The Bible, especially the New Testament, was opened up at that time. From that time onward, the Bible was no longer a locked-up book. It was not only an opened book but an interpreted book. It is sad, however, that most of Christianity at that time rejected the teaching of the Brethren. In addition, a number of ministries of the Word appeared among the Brethren themselves, and this brought in different opinions and caused divisions. By 1918, just after World War I, the Brethren had already been divided into hundreds of sects, and during the last forty years they have become even more divided. This division has almost completely annulled the Brethren. This is the real situation that we have witnessed.

THE HISTORY OF THE INTERPRETATION
OF THE WORD OF GOD

According to the situation we have observed, the understanding of the Word of God is desolate. In Christianity as a whole, the Bible is mostly still not opened or interpreted. Although at one time the Brethren had opened up the Bible, they eventually declined due to their internal tumults, disagreements, and serious contention regarding the truth. The United States has many seminaries, but today two in particular are considered as leaders in terms of theological teaching. One is Dallas Theological Seminary in Dallas, Texas; the other is Moody Bible Institute in Chicago, Illinois. Both of these receive the theological teachings of the Brethren.

Around 1900 the Scofield Reference Bible was very popular in the United States, and even today many people are still using it. More than ninety-five percent of the footnotes in this reference Bible originate from the theology and teachings of the Brethren. In other words, the footnotes are based on the light the Brethren saw from the Bible.

The light the Brethren saw from the Bible can be summarized by three main points. First, they saw the church in the New Testament. Beginning from them, people no longer regarded the church merely as a physical building. Before the Brethren were raised up, Christians in America and Europe generally believed that their chapels were the church. After the Brethren were raised up, however, they boldly declared that the church of God is not a chapel but an assembly that is called out by God. Because of this, they changed the word *church* to *assembly,* which means "a called-out congregation." What they taught was good, but what they saw was still too superficial. They did not see the intrinsic principle of life in the Body of Christ. They saw something concerning the Body and understood it a little. They realized that the Body of Christ is constituted with all the saved ones everywhere and at all times throughout the age of the Lord as the Spirit, but they did not thoroughly see the principles of life, resurrection, and the cross and the move of the Holy Spirit. Nevertheless, we were helped very much by the Brethren in the matter of the church.

Second, the Brethren saw the types in the Old Testament. Throughout the previous generations not one group of Christians had supplied a better interpretation of the types than the Brethren did. In this regard they helped us a great deal. However, after much in-depth study in the past few decades, we have seen something further that they did not see.

Third, they saw much related to the prophecies. Before the emergence of the Brethren, people in general were not clear about the second coming of the Lord Jesus. Some realized that the time of the resurrection of the Christians will be at the time of the coming of the Lord Jesus, but others said that the millennial kingdom would come when the gospel and truth have improved human society. People were not clear about the Lord Jesus' coming, nor did they fully understand the interpretation of the other prophecies in the Bible. Few people understood the prophecies in Daniel 2, 7, 8, 11, and 12 in a clear way, and there were even fewer who could open up the book of Revelation. It was the Brethren who opened up the book of Daniel, and they also opened up Revelation, at least on the surface. Although the Brethren were not accurate enough in many of the minor points, they did unlock something of what the Bible reveals concerning the church, the types, and the prophecies. However, only a portion of the true lovers and seekers of the Lord have accepted the teachings of the Brethren in the past one hundred sixty years.

USING THE WORD OF GOD
PROPERLY AND APPROPRIATELY

Today the Bible is in our hands, but I am afraid that the way to use it still remains a big question. Consider the many publications we have put out. According to the statistics, it takes someone at least four years to read through all of this material. It seems that all these riches are so abundant today that we do not know how to use them. When we go to lead and perfect a home meeting, we may not even know what kind of truth materials we have and how to use them. There are at least three to four kinds of materials for the edification of the new believers, but we need to decide which one to use. This shows us that to properly use spiritual materials is not an easy matter.

Moreover, we all have a heart to take the leading of the new way and go out to perfect the home meetings, but we find that the way to speak in a home meeting is a very difficult lesson to master. Speaking too much is not right, but neither is speaking too little. Speaking too profoundly may be unacceptable, but speaking too shallowly is not good, and speaking nothing is even worse. This causes us to be unsure about what to do; it is hard to find a principle to follow. The key to the matter depends on two things. First, we all need to be filled with the Holy Spirit and go out with the Spirit. Second, we need to be well-prepared with the Word. However, dealing with the Word is truly a problem. Our difficulty lies in how to use the Word of God properly. Once we use it properly, everything is fine.

Six thousand years of the development of human culture have produced an educational system that is commonly used throughout the whole world today. Education begins from kindergarten and continues through six years of elementary school, six years of middle and high school, and four years of university. Since this system is used worldwide, students who graduate locally can go to another country to further their education with more advanced research. This is the result of a scientific approach to education.

Spiritual education should be the same in principle, but where is our scientific approach? How can we arrange the truths in the Bible in a systematic way so that someone who has a heart to learn can enter into the depths in a simple way and study in a progressive, consistent, coherent, and logical way? If we can carry out such a way, this will be very good.

THE REASON FOR THE CHANGE OF THE SYSTEM

Christianity has been on the earth for two thousand years, and the truth in Christianity is unshakable. We can compare the truth of the Bible to the earth itself. Men can build bridges and roads, fly airplanes, and launch satellites into the sky, but no one can change the earth itself; it is God's creation, and there is no way to change it. The Bible cannot be changed; however, the way to interpret the Bible and use the Bible requires much consideration. In these two thousand years, no one has dared to make a definite conclusion regarding the proper way to meet and to preach the gospel, nor would anyone dare to say that he has been altogether successful in these matters. Even the giants of the gospel do not say that they are absolutely right. Therefore, even until now there is no definite way to preach the gospel. It is still in the stage of study and research.

It was not until the last few years that we definitely saw that the gospel of God and the salvation of God revealed in the Bible take the household as the unit. For example, Acts

16:31 says, "Believe on the Lord Jesus, and you shall be saved, you and your household," and Luke 19:9 says, "Today salvation has come to this house." It does not say that today salvation has come to this man, but to "this house." The types in the Old Testament also take the household as the unit. There were eight in Noah's household. He did not enter into the ark by himself, but his whole household entered (Gen. 7:1). At the Feast of the Passover, there was not a lamb for a person but a lamb for a household (Exo. 12:3). These all took the household as the unit.

The New Testament shows us that from the beginning the believers, who were brought in through the New Testament economy, had meetings in their homes, and they met from house to house. The Bible gives detailed descriptions of the content of the home meetings of the saints at that early stage. They were teaching in the homes, breaking bread in the homes, praying in the homes, fellowshipping in the homes, and preaching the gospel in the homes (Acts 2:42, 46; 5:42). Besides these five things, there was not much need of anything else in the Christian meetings. Although they still met in the synagogue, they may not have done it willingly, and there was no record of what they did there. In conclusion, it is clear that meeting in the homes is the most basic and complete way to meet. Because we have clearly seen this point, we changed the system that we have been practicing for years.

Meanwhile, we also saw that our former practices, though not absolutely according to the denominations, were not completely detached and different from the form and the element in the denominations. We can say that we are still much the same as they are. We have changed in form but not in content. Therefore, we have fallen into the same pitiful condition as the denominations. With regard to multiplication and propagation, our progress has been very slow. This is because we took the wrong way. If we were still using an ox cart to travel from Taipei to Kaohsiung, it would take at least two days to get there. In contrast, flying from Los Angeles to Taipei today requires only thirteen hours, which includes crossing thousands of miles over the Pacific Ocean. This illustrates why we must change our method and change the system.

In the past sixty years we have inherited and have been following the old way for too long and to too great an extent. To continue to conduct our meetings and preach the gospel according to the old way would be like going back to the ox cart. Not only is it outdated, but it is also unable to meet the need. However, changing one's nature is harder than changing mountains and rivers. It is hard for a man to change. We say that the ox cart is not good, but those who are accustomed to it still like to use it. They consider that taking the train is too troublesome; they say they are too limited by time and might miss the train. The ox cart, they say, is much more flexible; it is always available and can go and stop anywhere as one wishes. Yes, the ox cart has its advantages. We do not mean that the old way has no advantage at all, but when we compare the two ways, it is clear to us which way we should take.

LEARNING TO PRESENT THE TRUTH
CONCISELY TO OTHERS

We can apply the above matters practically in the following way. Whenever we fellowship in a home meeting, we must release our spirit every time we open our mouth. Whenever our spirit is released, we are not shy or fearful. We can compare this to a basketball game. Once the players get onto the field, they forget about heaven, earth, and even their own name. The only thing they know is to win the game. By being this way, they will surely win. Likewise, our spirit must be released. Second, before we go to lead a home meeting, we should have adequate prayer so that we will be bold in the release of the spirit. At the same time, we should also exercise to be equipped with the truth. If we exercise well enough, everything will become easy. We all should take heed to this point. Not only the young brothers and sisters but also the middle-aged and older ones should endeavor to exercise. This is the biggest lack in all of Christianity. There are many people who love and seek the Lord, but very few know how to lead others and what to do. This is due to the lack of exercise. I hope we can be strengthened in this matter.

The foremost thing is that we need to know the truth. This

is like teaching mathematics; if we are not good in mathematics, it is very difficult to teach it. The truth that we must know is first the truth concerning the church. We should help others to know the church in a thorough way. When we teach others, we need to make everything simple. Again we can compare this to a coach teaching his players. The coach first needs to teach them the basic movements, expecting that they would practice these basic matters thoroughly. When they play on the field, they do not need to perform every move that the coach taught them. They need only to apply them with flexibility according to the real situation with the goal of shooting the ball into the basket. I hope we all understand these two sides. On one side, we need to know and be equipped with the truth; on the other side, we need to speak the truth in a simplified and concise way, presenting it clearly to the new believers.

We can take the meaning of *church* as an example. The church is God's called-out assembly. In any place that there are believers like you and me coming together, there is God's called-out assembly. This is the first meaning of the church. If there is a need to explain the Greek text, we can simply mention that the word *church* in Greek means the "called-out assembly." In order to avoid difficulties, however, do not be overly concerned with using Greek. Second, the church is the Body of Christ. Everyone has a body. We all know that our human body is a composition and that it is not a lifeless organization. Rather, it is a living organism. The principle of the Body of Christ is the same as that of the organic members of our body. The key concept is the life within the body. Like our human body, the church as the organic Body of Christ is full of life within. The life of the Body of Christ is the life of God. On the other hand, a person's body is for expressing him. If a person has only a head but not a body, he has no expression. The body functions with the head to be an expression. The church is the organic expression of Christ. Therefore, the church is the fullness of Christ. Fullness is an overflow. If something does not overflow, it cannot be expressed. Once it overflows, the overflow becomes an expression.

ABANDONING THE SECTS

Every saved one should abandon the sects. Sects are parties which are formed into divisions. During earlier years in mainland China, some Christian groups liked to use the word *denomination,* as in "the Baptist denomination" and "the Presbyterian denomination." Later the Lord raised up the churches in the Lord's recovery as a testimony that denominations are a party formed into a sect. Galatians 5:19-20 says that sects are the work of the flesh. Paul condemns sects in 1 Corinthians 1, and God Himself condemns them. Since we "blew the trumpet" concerning sects, mainland China has been affected, and it is still affected to this today. Now many Christian groups no longer call themselves denominations. Although the word *denomination* sounds good on the surface, in reality it is condemned by many Christians. Therefore, they are not willing to use this term today.

Why should Christians not have sects? First, it is because Christ is not divided. We believe in one Lord. Christ is the unique One in the universe. Christ is the universal One and the eternal One. He is not divided, He cannot be divided, and He should not be divided. Paul asked the divisive ones, "Is Christ divided?" (1 Cor. 1:13). The answer certainly is in the negative: "No, Christ is not divided." Since Christ is not divided, we who believe into Him also should not be divided.

Second, the church is the Body of Christ. Everyone has only one body; the body of every human is unique. A person with two bodies would be a monster. Likewise, the Body of Christ is also unique. In Ephesians 4:4 Paul said, "One Body," in which is one Spirit. In this light we see that the Body is unique, and Christ cannot be divided. The Body of Christ, which is the church, is unique. Therefore, there is no ground, and there should be no ground for division.

Third, to divide Christians into religious sects is the work of the flesh. Galatians 5:19 says that the fruit, the works, of the flesh are manifest. Then Paul lists several items, one of which is sects. Where do sects come from? Verse 20 connects three things: factions, divisions, and sects. Initially there are factions and then divisions, which issue in the formation of sects. This is the condition of the whole of Christianity today. Without the shining of the light, people proudly claim that they belong to a certain group. Once the light shines, however, they see that these so-called groups are sects, which are condemned by God.

Sects are indicated in 1 Corinthians 1. The church in Corinth was an early church, raised up around A.D. 50. By the time 1 Corinthians was written, it was already in a condition of division. This means that shortly after this church was established, it was divided into different groups. What was the basis of their divisions? The divisions were according to the persons who led them. Some preferred Paul, so they were "of" Paul; some preferred Cephas, so they were "of" Cephas; and some preferred Apollos, so they were "of" Apollos. Thus, the church was divided into at least three groups. Still others said that those were wrong and that Christ was best, so they were "of" Christ; eventually four groups were formed. In rebuking them, Paul seemed to say, "Is Christ divided? Why do you say that you are of Paul? Was Paul crucified for you? It was not I who was crucified for you; it was Christ who was crucified for you. Or were you baptized into the name of Paul? No, you all were baptized into the name of Christ. Therefore, none of you should be 'of' me."

Then in 3:21-22 Paul seemed to tell them, "Do not say that you are of me. Rather, I, Paul, am yours, for all things are yours, including me." Paul strictly condemned the sects. In 1:10 Paul said, "That there be no divisions among you," and in Titus 3:10 he also said, "A factious man, after a first and second admonition, refuse." He pointed out clearly that we should reject and not encourage or promote factions. As a result, there should not be factions among Christians; that is, there should be no sects.

THE FORMATION OF SECTS

Special Creeds

What is a sect, and what constitutes a sect? There are three obvious items in a sect. First, it has a special creed; second, it has a special fellowship; and third, it has a special name. These three "specials" can be found in almost all the groups in Christianity today. For instance, the Baptist Church strongly emphasizes baptism by immersion in water. We all know that baptism is in the Bible, but to make it a special designation, that is, to make it a special creed, is not of the Bible. The Baptist Church not only requires people to be baptized, but they also emphasize that people must be baptized in their church and in their water and that other baptisms do not count. If someone has already been baptized and wants to attend the meetings in the Baptist Church, he will have to be baptized again by them. This is according to a special creed, which is a matter of their faith which one must follow. As a result, a sect has been produced.

All those who are saved have a common faith. The common faith is this: First, in this universe there is only one God, who is self-existing and ever-existing, who created the heavens and the earth, and who is the Father, the Son, and the Spirit. Second, God in the Son one day became flesh to be a man. He died on the cross to accomplish redemption for us and was buried. On the third day He resurrected to bring life to us. He then ascended to the heavens, and in heaven He exercises His power for the preaching of the gospel to save sinners and to produce the church on the earth. At the end of this age He will come back again to gather those who have believed into Him. This is our common, fundamental faith. What issues from this common faith is the producing of the church.

To make a special creed out of any condition or matter other than this common faith, even if such a matter is in the Bible, eventually forms a sect. Some Christians were baptized not by immersion but by sprinkling, and some even passed through the flag-waving ceremony of the Salvation Army. No one can say that these people have not believed. Like us, they also hold the common faith of the Triune God, the redemptive death of the Lord Jesus, and His resurrection and ascension. Their distinction is only that they were not baptized by immersion. The Baptist Church treats this belief as a special creed, which has caused them to become a sect.

Special Fellowship

In accordance with their special creed, the Baptist Church,

for example, has a certain fellowship among themselves. This is a special fellowship. Whenever a Baptist Church is about to take the Lord's supper, someone may make an announcement that those who are not members of that church have to leave. This practice indicates a special fellowship. The Presbyterian Church also has their special fellowship, in which the church is administered by elders. They emphasize this even to the extent that they take the administration of the elders as their name. Theirs is a special creed, and this special creed has produced a special fellowship.

Special Names

Some say that they are of the Baptist Church, while others say they are of the Presbyterian, Lutheran, Methodist, Anglican, or Episcopalian Church. When you drive through Orange County in Southern California, you may see a sign that says, "The American Anglican Church," and not long after that you may see another sign that says, "The Taiwanese Church in Orange County." This is truly saddening. All these special names completely divide the children of God.

All these special names are considered as a sin in the Bible. My own wife should be called Mrs. Lee. To name herself Mrs. Cheung, for example, would be a serious problem. Likewise, the church belongs to Christ. How can it be named the Lutheran Church or the Methodist Church? All these names are wrong. Any name other than the name of Christ is not only divisive but indicates a spiritual sin before God. Therefore, we should not have special creeds, special fellowships, or special names.

We should endeavor to keep the oneness of the Body of Christ. This oneness of the Body is the oneness of the Spirit in Ephesians 4:3. The Spirit who dwells in us is the oneness. As long as we walk according to the Spirit, we will have oneness. But when we do not walk according to the Spirit, differences are produced. The situation in today's Christianity is mainly due to these three matters—special creeds, special fellowships, and special names. All those who take these three items commit the same transgression of ignoring the Spirit. If all the children of God were to care for the Spirit and walk according to the Spirit, there would be no special creeds, special fellowships, or special names, and spontaneously we all would be one. Our oneness is the Spirit.

A CONCLUDING WORD

When we go to perfect a home meeting, we should not be rigid and unchanging; we need to be flexible. In perfecting people, we need to know their condition. For instance, some people may have been baptized by us, but they were taken away by the denominations. Or some may have thought that they should attend a "service" on the Lord's Day, so they went by themselves to a certain chapel of a certain group. If this is their condition, we need to receive the Lord's leading to help them see that the church belongs to Christ and that Christ cannot be divided. The church is the Body of Christ and is unique. Then we should lead them to read the Bible to see that division is fleshy and condemned by God and that we should reject it completely.

We also have to teach them that any group that has a special creed, special fellowship, or special name is a sect. We should discard all these things and follow the Spirit in keeping the oneness of the Body of Christ. This is the proper situation of the church. I believe that the new ones will receive help from this kind of fellowship.

(A message given on March 12, 1987 in Taipei, Taiwan)

CHAPTER NINE

BEING A WITNESS TO BEAR FRUIT

THE LIFE SUPPLY FOR THE NEW BELIEVERS

According to our study and observation, we feel that we still need to prepare a set of materials for the perfecting of the home meetings. This set of materials will be specifically for the new believers in the first year of their Christian life. It should be not only concise but also practical. We hope to help the new ones to get into *Life Lessons* immediately after they are baptized. We believe that they will be perfected in many ways by the supply in these materials, and they will be helped to receive the various truths in the Bible.

BEING A WITNESS OF THE LORD'S LIFE TO BEAR FRUIT

On the one hand, a person who serves the Lord should have outward activities and work, but on the other hand, he should never forget that all work must come from the inner life. Without life, all work is empty and vain. Only life is the content and reality of our work. Therefore, we must work for God and bear fruit, while on the other hand, we must be witnesses of the Lord's life. Apparently, to be a witness does not have much to do with life, but in actuality to be a witness is to bear witness for life. Being a witness is not a work but a testimony of life.

CHRIST, HAVING PASSED THROUGH
DEATH AND RESURRECTION,
BEING THE WONDERFUL ONE IN THE UNIVERSE

As we all know, the Gospels speak of a person, Jesus Christ. After passing through death and resurrection, this person wrought Himself into those who believed into Him.

Those whom we see at the end of the Gospels, the ones who followed the Lord Jesus for three and a half years, were the ones into whom the Lord entered after His death and resurrection. The end of the Gospel of John tells us that the Lord Jesus, after passing through death and resurrection, came into the midst of these disciples. No one can understand the way He came. At that time the disciples were in a room with closed doors and windows, yet He entered with a resurrected body. He was able to do this only because He was the Spirit. However, we should not say that He was only the Spirit, because He came also with a resurrected body. He entered into the closed room with a resurrected body, came into the midst of the disciples, and breathed into them, saying, "Receive the Holy Spirit" (20:22). From that day on, He breathed Himself into them. In this way He and the disciples became one. This is a wonderful matter.

From its beginning, the Gospel of John tells us that the Lord Jesus is God, He is the Word of God, and He became flesh and lived on this earth. After this He went to the cross to be crucified, and He was resurrected. In His resurrection He became the wonderful One. We can say that this wonderful One is God, but He is also a man. We can say that He is a man, but He has a body not of the old creation but of the new creation and of resurrection. We cannot clearly explain how He was able to come in and out of a room with the doors and windows shut. He could show His body to the disciples, yet He was a Spirit. This is indeed wonderful. We cannot understand this with our human mentality. There are many things in the universe that we do not understand and cannot explain to others. Among them the most wonderful thing is the resurrected Jesus. We cannot say that He is not physical, because He has a body which the disciples could touch, with the mark of the nails and the wound from the spear in His side. He was physical and could be touched, yet He freely went in and out of a room that was closed, and He even breathed Himself into those who believed into Him. These things are difficult for anyone to understand, yet they are recorded in the Bible.

These wonderful things happened at the end of the Gospel of John. After that, the book of Acts begins. Acts records how the Christ who passed through death and resurrection and entered into the disciples lived and moved with the disciples for a period of forty days. Sometimes He was hidden, and sometimes He appeared to them. He came and left, left and came again. In reality, however, He did not come and leave. Rather, He appeared and hid Himself, then hid Himself and appeared again. He was omnipresent. Sometimes He appeared, but sometimes He was hidden. He appeared in the upper room, and He also appeared outside the room. However, after people saw Him in His appearing, He became hidden again. This was to prove that this Christ who died and resurrected had already entered into His disciples in His resurrection. He was already in the disciples, but from the disciples' point of view, He was sometimes visible and sometimes invisible; sometimes they could feel Him, but other times they could not feel anything. He was indeed a wonderful One, for He is the Spirit and the reality.

Today the Lord is the same to us. This is hard for us to explain, but it is a fact that He is in us. Sometimes we sense His coming, and sometimes we sense His leaving. Sometimes we feel that He is here, and sometimes we feel that He is not here. This is our inner story, and we all have this experience.

A WITNESS OF THE LORD
BEING ONE WHO HAS DIED AND RESURRECTED

In Acts 1, the disciples who personally observed the Lord's death and resurrection immediately became witnesses of the Lord. Verse 8 says, "You shall be My witnesses...unto the uttermost part of the earth." By this we see that the Lord Jesus wanted the disciples to go out not to do a work but to be a certain kind of person. What kind of person should they be? They should be witnesses of Christ. To be a witness is not to go to court to testify of things you have seen and heard or to give details of a particular story. Rather, to be a witness means that the person for whom you are witnessing has become you, and you have become Him. Your going is His going; your being there is His being there. You are there to be His witness.

It is not easy for Christians to understand the Bible, and it is even harder to comprehend spiritual things. In the matter of being the Lord's witnesses, we often like to say, "We need to witness for the Lord." This saying is not accurate. As witnesses of the Lord, we often think that we need to give a good testimony for Him, testifying to people how lovely, real, reliable, and powerful our Savior is. However, such an understanding is not proper. Today we are the Lord's witnesses, testifying nothing other than the Lord's death and resurrection.

In fact, a witness of the Lord is one who has died and resurrected. When the Lord Jesus was on the earth, every day He lived a life of death and resurrection. He said, "The words that I say to you I do not speak from Myself, but the Father who abides in Me does His works" (John 14:10b). In other words, the Lord did not speak from Himself but from the Father. This means that the Father spoke His word through the Lord. This is the meaning of death and resurrection. To experience genuine death and resurrection means that a person lives not by himself but by putting himself aside. In other words, he puts himself to death. As the Lord put Himself to death, the One who was in Him was lived out. It is the same with us. Only when we put ourselves to death can the Lord Jesus be lived out from us.

The two—the Lord and the Father—are one. The Lord said that He was in the Father, and the Father was in Him (v. 10a). His speaking was the Father's working in Him. His speaking was not His own, but He spoke what the Father spoke. When He spoke, it was the Father who was speaking in Him. Therefore, He and the Father not only lived one living, but they also lived by one life; the two were one. This is very hard to explain, but it is the same with us today. The Lord and we, we and He, are living one living and are living by one life. Therefore, we can say that it is no longer I but Christ (Gal. 2:20). This is the meaning of death and resurrection. It is no longer we. Our old man has died. Now it is Christ who lives in us. He and we, the two, are just one.

The Lord Jesus never acted alone in the Gospels. He said that the Father never left Him, but the Father was with Him all the time (John 8:29). He never spoke by Himself, worked by Himself, or acted by Himself. All His moving was one with the Father. His move was the Father's move, and His speaking was the Father's speaking. All that He did was the expression of the Father, so the two were one. The Lord Himself always stood in death, and once He stood in death, the Father was able to live out from within Him.

When the Lord Jesus began His ministry, the first thing He did was to be baptized. Baptism denotes death and burial. Through baptism, the Lord Jesus proclaimed to man that He needed to die and be buried. He came out to work not by Himself but by the Father. Therefore, He needed to die and be buried and let the Father live in Him. From that day onward, these two—the Father and the Son—were one life and had one living. The man Jesus Christ lived a life of dying, and God the Father lived out from Him. This was the Lord's living of death and resurrection. He did not wait until His crucifixion to pass through death and resurrection. In fact, He died and resurrected daily while He was living on the earth for thirty-three and a half years. In principle, He always said, "Father,...not as I will, but as You will" (Matt. 26:39). *Not as I will* implies that the Lord was dying, while *but as You will* denotes that the Father was lived out. This is the meaning of death and resurrection.

We who serve the Lord today, either to go out to knock on doors or to perfect the home meetings, must see the truth expressed as, "I have died, and it is Christ who lives in me." Paul said that we who serve the Lord die daily so that we may no longer live to ourselves but to Him who died for us and has been raised (2 Cor. 5:15). This means that we die, and He lives. This is death and resurrection. This is not an exchange of two persons, an exchanged life. Rather, this is the joining of two lives, as in grafting. To graft a branch into a tree is to join the two lives together. One is eliminated, and the other one is lived out. The result is that the two lives join together as one life.

ALWAYS FOLLOWING THE SPIRIT
AND LIVING AND WALKING IN THE LORD

If we pay too much attention to the number of people and to the outward activities in the church life, I am afraid that we will all become "athletes" who know only how to run a race; that is, that we will have only physical activities without functioning in spirit. If this continues, we will all become like robots, moving when the machinery moves and not moving when it stops. We may pray for twenty minutes before going out for door-knocking, and our prayers may be thorough. Moreover, we may truly be filled in our prayer and have the feeling that the Spirit is with us in our going. In spite of this, what worries me the most is that the Spirit is with us only at the time we pray. When we go out to knock on doors, our going may become a mere activity.

We must remember that we are not the ones who cause people to receive life. We may baptize people, but we cannot give them life. We must learn that it is no longer I but Christ. It is not I who goes door-knocking, who speaks, and who baptizes people, but it is Christ. Everything is Christ. We must use our spirit and exercise the life and faith within us, declaring to God and to all the enemies in the universe, "It is not I who goes door-knocking, but it is Christ who goes. It is not I who speaks to people, but it is Christ who speaks. It is not I who causes people to believe, but it is Christ who does it. It is not even I who baptizes people, but it is Christ who baptizes them." If we have such an attitude, such a spirit, such a life, and such a faith, we will live a life that is always dependent on Him.

Depending on Him in this way moment by moment is our abiding in the Lord. When the Lord Jesus was on the earth, He abode in the Father day by day. He was never detached from the Father. His move was the Father's move, and His speaking was the Father's speaking. Today as we are serving the Lord, we must exercise to the extent that our going is the Lord's going, and our move is the Lord's move. At that time we will realize that we are not alone. Instead, it is the Lord and we together, two spirits joining as one spirit and two lives joining as one life. Although our body acts, visits people, goes door-knocking, and baptizes people, our spirit is joined to the Lord as one spirit.

We need to exercise to be joined to the Lord as one spirit and pray all the time, "O Lord, I have no way to impart life into others, but this is what You can do and should do. Lord, I rely on You in doing this. You and I have become one spirit. As I am here baptizing people, it is Your Spirit who baptizes people into the Triune God. Lord, I can only put a man into a bathtub and immerse him in water, but I have no way to baptize him into the Triune God. Only Your Spirit can do this. Thank you, Lord, that You and I have become one spirit. Whenever I am moving here, it is You who moves." This is the faith we should exercise to have.

We also need to walk according to the spirit. Although we have received some training, we still need to follow the spirit when we go out. Sometimes we think that we should do something in a certain way, but the spirit within us directs us in a different way. We must follow the spirit immediately and walk according to the spirit. In this way, everything we do will have the spirit as its base and life as its content.

BAPTIZING PEOPLE IN A SERIOUS WAY

According to our observation, there is the danger that when we go door-knocking to lead people to salvation and baptize them, what we do may become "mechanical." This may be due to the fact that our spirit is not strong enough and that we do not want to exercise our spirit. Due to the training that we have received in the past, we have become very experienced in door-knocking and baptizing people, even to the extent that our wealth of experience has become a mechanical method. The result is that there is not much life and spirit in what we do.

Consider our practice of baptism. I believe that many of us have the feeling that when we go door-knocking and baptize people, our way is sometimes too careless. We do not take this matter seriously, nor do we impress people deeply with baptism. Baptism is a matter that concerns man's coming out of death and entering into life, coming out of the world and entering into God's kingdom, and coming out of the self and entering into the Triune God. Hence, it is a very serious matter.

We need to see that going out to baptize people is a great matter. If we had other options, we would prefer not to baptize anyone in a bathtub but in a pool or a stream. Nevertheless, we must still take it seriously and give the baptized ones the feeling that this is a very important matter, a matter that concerns their being delivered from perdition to salvation and their coming out of death and entering into life. This is a life-changing matter—they are coming out of themselves and entering into the Triune God—and we should give people this feeling. If we baptize them in a loose manner, giving them a poor feeling, they will avoid us on our next visit.

If there are any special needs that arise from our door-knocking, we should have fellowship right away so that the situation can be studied without delay. For example, some young people accepted the gospel and were baptized while their parents were not at home. Then their parents returned home, and they were forced to give up the gospel. When we next visited them, their parents refused to let them open the door. This is understandable, and we were forced to accept their decision. Another situation arose when a husband was not home during our visit. The wife believed in the Lord and was baptized, but when her husband returned home, he annulled her faith. When we visited them again, she kept the door shut. This also is understandable, and we were forced to accept it. In a third kind of situation, we baptized certain ones, but afterward some from Christianity contacted them and led them away before our next visit. This situation is also understandable, although not entirely acceptable, because it shows that we did not adequately protect and care for the new ones. A newborn baby needs to be protected the moment he comes out of his mother's womb. If we protect him, he will survive; if we do not protect him, he will die. What happened with these new ones is yet another kind of situation in which people do not like to see us, lose confidence in us and respect for us, and reject us due to our improper approach. We need to be greatly adjusted in these matters.

Because we have never taken the new way before, we need to study it as we go on. We can compare this to following a car. If the car in front comes across a problem on the road, it can report the road conditions to the cars behind. Then they can consider what to do. In the same way, when we go to knock on doors, baptize others, or perfect the home meetings, we should follow the principle that we fellowship immediately whenever we discover a difficulty. Then we can discuss the way to deal with the problem in a proper manner. If we do not have fellowship when we discover difficulties, but instead discuss them in private, we are simply gossiping, which is neither appropriate nor proper.

I hope that from now on we will be particularly alert when we go out to baptize people. We must never be careless or casual. Instead, we must be very serious. We should never act rashly in order to save time. We should rather spend a little more time and baptize them in a respectable and serious manner. Even though a person may be baptized in a bathtub, our attitude must still be serious. We should fill the tub in a proper manner, accompany him to prepare and change clothes in a proper manner, and have clear fellowship with him to help him to realize that he has been saved. If we do this in a serious manner, the newly saved one will have a deep impression about his baptism. He too will respect it and be serious about it.

We should tell those who are being baptized that baptism is a very significant matter. It is the reality of coming out of death into life, coming out of darkness into light, and being saved from Satan's hand and entering into the kingdom of the Son of God's love. From then on, they will be in the grace of God, enjoying God's full salvation. This kind of speaking will edify them and give them a serious feeling toward baptism. At the same time, we need to explain to them the significance of water in baptism so that they can understand its meaning. We should believe that when we are serious, our words will certainly be of the spirit, having reality and power to impress people. When people are baptized in this way, they will have this impression: "I am a different person now. I have come out of death and entered into life, and I have been delivered from Satan and entered into the kingdom of the Son of God's love." In this way, it will not be easy for other people to damage them. Parents may obstruct and husbands may restrict, but within the ones we contact there will be a clear realization that they have been baptized and that a reality has entered into them. This is something that they will not be able ever to forget for the rest of their lives.

We must pay special attention to a particular matter. If there is no bathtub in a person's home, we should never simply sprinkle him with water. This way is too careless and casual. We would rather not baptize him at that moment but make an appointment with him for another time at another place in order to baptize him in a serious manner. We should never be careless about baptism lest people have a dubious impression of us. These are areas in which we should be careful and cautious.

Regardless of whether we knock on doors to baptize people or go to perfect a home meeting, we should act and move in the principle of death and resurrection, living in the spirit and following the spirit. We need to leave people with the impression that these matters are very significant and serious.

A QUESTION AND ANSWER

Question: Can we affect someone's thought about baptism by speaking more to him about it?

Answer: With whatever organ you speak to people, that organ in others will be touched. If you speak to people with your spirit, you will touch their spirit. If you speak to them with your mind, you will touch their mind. Moreover, if you speak to them with a suspicious, analytical, and argumentative tone, you will stir up a debate. It all depends on you. We must exercise our spirit and learn to speak in the spirit, telling people, "Dear friends, this is a great matter. This is the day that you can 'walk out of hell.'" When we speak in this way, the Spirit will work in them. If we ask them in the mind, "Do you know that today is the day that you are walking out of hell?", they will answer, "No, I don't." Hence, it matters how we speak. We must speak from our spirit and give others the feeling that our speaking is in the attitude of the spirit, the tone of the spirit, and is not merely from our mind. We should realize that the attitude and the tone of our mind only stir up debate.

We must never baptize people in a loose manner. This is

improper. We should not care about the number of people we baptize each day. This does not depend on what we think; rather, it depends on the work of the Holy Spirit. If the Holy Spirit saves one person, we will baptize one. If He saves ten people, we will baptize ten. How many will be baptized is not up to us. Rather, it is up to the Holy Spirit and the cooperation of the environment.

With regard to idol worship, we must have a time of clear fellowship with the newly saved ones that since they have believed in the Lord, they should forsake all the idols. If they do not forsake the idols, the Lord cannot accept them. We cannot baptize those who are not willing to reject the idols. If they say that they want to reject the idols, we should help them to smash them. The idols must be done away with. However, we do not necessarily need to resolve matters such as smoking and drinking right away, because both smoking and drinking are a kind of habit. To deal with these requires the newly saved ones to overcome by the Lord's life after their baptism. Idols, however, need to be dealt with right away.

(A message given on March 17, 1987 in Taipei, Taiwan)

CHAPTER TEN

TWO BASIC ELEMENTS FOR
THE PERFECTING OF HOME MEETINGS—
THE SPIRIT AND THE WORD

There are many aspects that we should pay attention to in perfecting the home meetings. Of these, the most important ones—the ones which enable people to be perfected in life, which supply life and cause people to grow in life—are the Spirit and the word. The Spirit is the Spirit of the Lord, and the word is the word of the Lord. The Spirit must be strong, and the word must be rich. Although we have paid much attention to these two aspects in the past, we are human and are still in our flesh, our natural feelings, and our natural thoughts. Even if we have been serving the Lord with our full time for a long time, our practice related to the Spirit and the word is still lacking.

OPINIONS BEING THE SOURCE OF CONFUSION
IN THE CHURCH

Although the church has been on the earth for over two thousand years, it has borne little testimony for the Lord. Rather, it has borne much confusion and divisions stemming from confusion. This is why Christians today are divided into sects and denominations. All the sects and denominations come out of opinions, which are the root of all divisions. Every person has opinions, regardless of how knowledgeable he is or what his social status is. Only a man made of wood or stone would have no opinions. We have met many people. Some are high-class, while some are low-class. They are civilized or uncivilized, well-educated or uneducated, capable or incapable, but none of them is without opinions. An employer has opinions, and so do his employees. A teacher has opinions, and so do the students; parents have opinions, and children have even more opinions. There is not a single person who is without opinions.

I hope that we would drop our own opinions and not bring them into the church. Once we allow opinions to come in, we will not only harm ourselves but cause trouble for others. Hence, we should not keep our opinions. As soon as opinions come in, all our previous work will be wasted. Not only our own efforts but even the efforts of all those who have been serving us in the church will be brought to naught.

We must realize that all the divisions in Christianity are the result of opinions. Over sixty years ago, the Lord raised up His recovery among us. As a rule, in the recovery there are the Spirit, the truth, and life. We should be able to stand on the foundation of the Spirit, the truth, and life and go forward. To our shame, however, there have not been much multiplication and increase among us over the past sixty years. What is the reason behind this? The reason is our opinions. Although we are not large in number, everyone has opinions. Time and again I have seen people come in and leave due to the same reason, that is, due to opinions. Even in the days of Brother Nee the situation was the same, and he had no way to deal with it.

Brother Nee was one who never argued with others. When others did not argue with him, he was able to speak freely to supply them. However, when people argued with him, he preferred not to utter a word. I have witnessed people coming to him to plead with him many times, but he simply would smile and keep silent. After one such incident, I asked him why he refused to speak. He replied, "Even if I had spoken, he would not have listened to me. He came to seek approval from me for his opinions. If I were to agree with his opinions, I would be doing him harm, but if I were to disagree and say something else, he would not have been willing to listen to me. Therefore, what is the point of my speaking?" This was his attitude. By this we can see that it is difficult to deal with people who are absorbed in their own opinions.

During the first five or six years after the Lord's recovery came to Taiwan, from 1949 to about 1955, all the brothers and sisters on the island were truly in one accord, just as Romans 15:5-6 says, "Be of the same mind...with one accord...with one mouth." The number of people in the churches increased one hundredfold within those five or six years. Before that time, there were only about four to five hundred brothers and sisters in the whole of Taiwan, from Taipei to Kaohshiung, but after those years the number increased to forty or fifty thousand. It was a pity, however, that some among us were seeking after so-called "spirituality," which produced many opinions. Eventually, these ones invited a well-known evangelist from abroad, whose arrival brought even more opinions into the church.

This brother strongly disagreed with the practice of the church, particularly with the establishment of church meetings in one locality after another. According to his opinion, he wanted to establish his own ministry in order to gain a group of people through the messages he released. This group of people would stand with him, but they need not establish a meeting around him; they could still return to their various denominations and work secretly in their midst. Hence, this brother and his group of followers became the most unwelcome people among the denominations. This is because the denominations knew that they actually had another motive even though they appeared to be meeting happily with the believers.

This brother opposed the ground of the church to the uttermost, and he came to us with the intention to overturn this ground. He told people very clearly that the ground of the church was heretical and mistaken. He even wrote a letter to the young people among us expressing his opinions. From this you can see how strong this brother's opinions were! This incident ushered in a big turmoil among us around 1960. From that time on, the one accord among the churches in Taiwan was never recovered to what it used to be before 1954. Doctors know that once damage has been done to the body, it is very difficult to recover it to its original condition.

During the years between 1949 and 1954, all of us were of one heart and one mouth, sharing the same burden and the same goal. At that time, we did not hear any opinions, whether we were at a co-workers' meeting, church meeting, or training meeting. Not a single person expressed any opinions. Instead, everyone received the Lord's leading among us, and this eventually brought in God's blessing. Around 1960, though, this turmoil was stirred up by that particular opinion with the result of inflicting great damage on our spirit. Of course, we also realized that Satan's fiery darts are always directed at the leading ones, and the leading ones will always be the target of Satan's attacks.

Later the Lord's recovery came to the United States. The truth concerning life was released with much revelation. Not a single message was empty or meaningless; all the messages were full of the light of life and the supply of life. Because of this, they were very much welcomed by those who loved the Lord and pursued Him with a pure heart. Therefore, during the first twenty years the situation among us was overwhelmingly positive. At that time the Lord's recovery spread across the whole of America, from the east to the west and from the north to the south. Although our numbers were not very large, there were still a number of saints who were raised up to follow this ministry, to take the way of the recovery ordained by God, and to go on according to the revelation of His divine word by the supply of life in His word. At that time, there were no opinions in the church.

However, this good condition did not last for long. Opinions gradually emerged. There were some brothers who were regarded as proper, honest, and without guile, and they had some thorough fellowship with us. Nevertheless, they began to have opinions. They felt that the way to build up the local churches under our leading was not the most excellent way. Rather, they felt that their way was the most excellent way, but what they considered to be excellent was entirely contrary to the scriptural way. One example was their opinion about the breaking of bread. They overemphasized the correct time for breaking the bread, and they stressed the "universality" of the breaking of bread. This means that everyone, including adults, children, toddlers, and even babies should receive a share of the bread. They claimed that this was the most excellent way to build up the local churches. Due to their strong opinions they left in 1974, and a small group of others left with them. Such circumstances weakened the Lord's recovery.

RECEIVING ONE LEADING WITH ONE ACCORD

Over the years, we have seen the danger brought about by opinions in various localities. For this reason we have held several trainings to present again the truth of the divine revelation. We believe that the truth is unalterable, like the multiplication tables in mathematics. Two times two is four; no one can change it at will to be more or less. The numbers are fixed and cannot be altered. Likewise, as long as the truth is presented, it will prevail.

We do not allow any room for opinions in our training. If you have opinions, please do not come to the training. If you cannot drop your opinions in the training, we would ask you to withdraw. If we hold on to our opinions, the training will be a waste of effort; the opinions and the effort will offset one other. The truth that we speak and the instructions that we give have all undergone a long period of research and study. We hope that everyone will receive them with a humble heart, drop his own opinions, and go on with one accord.

In the first twelve chapters of the book of Acts, we see Peter as the main leading one among the churches. We cannot see any opinions at that time. In the latter part of the book of Acts, from chapters thirteen to twenty-eight, Paul was in the lead, and again we mostly do not find opinions. However, in Acts 21 James had certain opinions when Paul arrived at Jerusalem. James told Paul, "You observe, brother, how many thousands there are among the Jews who have believed." Then he went on to speak concerning the multitude of the Jews. On the one hand, they believed in Jesus, but on the other hand, they also kept the law of Moses. When they heard that Paul had taught people throughout the nations not to keep the law of Moses, they were deeply troubled. Hence, James felt that there was a need for Paul to clarify his standing to them (vv. 20-25). In this example we see James's opinions.

The Bible tells us that it was because of this opinion that Paul was arrested and put in prison. On the surface Paul's imprisonment appeared to be negative, but in actuality it was

God's salvation, rescuing him from the chaotic situation in Jerusalem. It was for this reason that Paul was sent to Rome. Some years later in A.D. 70, God destroyed the entire city of Jerusalem through Titus and his Roman army. The church in Jerusalem and all that belonged to the church were completely destroyed. This reveals to us how terrible opinions can be.

Therefore, we have "sounded the trumpet." In this ministry we have only one leading without any opinions. However, this does not mean that everyone in the Lord's recovery has to receive this leading. Certainly not! If someone receives this leading, he is in the Lord's recovery, and if he does not receive it, he is still in the Lord's recovery. This sounding of the trumpet is similar to that of Gideon in Judges 7. In the Old Testament Gideon came out to sound the trumpet for the sake of fighting the battle, but not every Israelite was able or willing to follow. Many people came to Gideon, but God told him that he could not use them all and that he had to test their true condition by their drinking of water. Eventually, God chose only three hundred among them. Gideon took this three hundred with him, won the battle, and saved the Israelites. Our deep burden is to sound the trumpet to all of you in the hope of gaining those who will be like the three hundred warriors who went with Gideon. Everyone should hear only one calling and receive one leading without any opinions.

Experience tells us that things often start off well, but gradually as opinions creep in, the situation changes. This is terrible and very dangerous. We must realize that what has caused divisions in Christianity is nothing other than opinions. It is opinions that have frustrated the Lord's work, causing Him to have no way on the earth. Consider the Lord's work on the earth today. There is absolutely no way for the Lord in Protestantism and Catholicism. In their early days the Brethren saw the truth in the Bible. The Bible was no longer closed but gradually was opened, made clear, and illuminated. However, less than two centuries later they became divided into more than a thousand separated groups. This was the result of opinions. The Lord's recovery has been on the earth for sixty to seventy years, and it faces the same problem of opinions which have frustrated the Lord's work and limited His multiplication and increase on the earth.

For this reason, it is important especially for all the young people who take the way of the Lord's recovery to learn the lesson of not expressing their opinions loosely. We must realize that the recovery has had more than sixty years of history on the earth. It has passed through many obstacles, turmoils, and sufferings. During these years, there have also been much research and study. While we cannot say that we have exhausted all the Christian publications, we have at least studied in great depth the important church histories, autobiographies, and core messages in Christianity. We have also thoroughly studied the ways to practice the church life. What we are doing today is presenting, to those who seek the Lord out of a pure heart, the things that we have learned, the things that we have come to know, and the things that the Lord has commissioned us with, as well as the revelation and vision that we have received from His word.

THE SPIRIT OF GOD AND THE WORD OF GOD BEING ABLE TO SUPPLY LIFE

In the past we presented thirty items concerning the training of our character. Each point causes our soul to be subdued, submissive, and restrained in order that we may mature. We often describe a certain person as being "barbaric" to indicate that his character has not been properly trained. Man consists of three parts—spirit, soul, and body. All these parts need to undergo much training. However, when we go out to minister life to others, the source of supply does not depend on our perfect physique, our trained and non-barbaric soul, or even the condition of our human spirit. Our going out to minister life to others altogether hinges on the Spirit of God and the word of God.

We must pay attention to the Spirit of God and the word of God regardless of how old or young we are. How much ground the Spirit of God has within us, the condition of the Spirit of God in us, and how much we are being equipped and perfected with the word of God are the secrets to our ministering life to others. Many in Christianity often think that the prevailing of the Lord's work in the age of the apostles was due to the power of the Holy Spirit. This is somewhat the case, but if we study Acts carefully, we will find out that it is not only the Spirit of God that is mentioned; the word of God is mentioned as well. Everyone seems to think that the most important matter in the book of Acts is the Spirit of God. They do not realize that the word of God is also very important.

There are three portions in the book of Acts that speak in the same way. Acts 6:7 says, "The word of God grew," and 12:24 says, "But the word of God grew." Then again 19:20 says, "The word of the Lord grew mightily and prevailed." However, we cannot find a verse in Acts saying that the power of the Holy Spirit resulted in an increase in the number of people in the church. Instead, it says that the word of God flourished, multiplied, increased, and greatly prevailed.

The problem in Christianity is with opinions, and the poverty in Christianity is due to the lack of the word of God. When we visit various groups of Christians today, we find that there is a great lack of the word of God. Even among those who have the proper interpretation of the word in the Bible, what is spoken is often shallow and superficial. Many have not seen the profound truth and revelation of God and the eternal economy of God that are revealed in the Bible. They have a great lack as far as the word is concerned.

Christianity has become a religion, an organization, that practices the clergy-laity system and cares for rituals and regulations but does not have much of the word of God. At a certain point, the charismatic movement was raised up because some people felt that Christianity was short of the Holy Spirit and the power of the Spirit. These people greatly promoted and publicized, in every possible human way, the outpouring of the Holy Spirit, speaking in tongues, miracles, and so forth. Although they have close to two hundred years of history, their numbers remain small. What is the reason for this? It is because they too do not have much of the word of God.

It Being the Spirit that Gives Life

Today the life-pulse of the Lord's recovery is the word of

the Lord. But to have only the word of the Lord without the Spirit is like having the outward shell of a body without the inward content of life. This is emptiness. Thus, the word and the Spirit must work together. There must be the word of the Lord as well as the Spirit of the Lord. We must keep ourselves in a condition in which we have continuous fellowship with the Lord. We should spend at least twenty minutes each day to come before the Lord to contact Him, to empty ourselves, and to deal with ourselves thoroughly so that He can possess our entire being and so that the Holy Spirit can fill all of our inward parts. Moreover, we should exercise to remain in such a state throughout our daily living. This will keep us in union with the Spirit of the Lord.

The Word Supplying Life
and Causing the Growth in Life

On the other hand, we must be equipped with the word of the Lord. In particular, we need to have an in-depth knowledge of the New Testament. We should endeavor to be soaked in the word of the Lord and to let the word saturate us so that we have the word of the Lord within and without in order to cooperate with His Spirit. In this way, when we go out to perfect a home meeting, it will not matter much whether or not we have prepared any materials. As long as we are those who are full of the Spirit of God and the word of God, we will be able to supply life to others through our singing, praying, and reading the Scriptures with them. On the contrary, if we take this fellowship as a mere regulation, the result will be that there is no Spirit or life.

We have received the New Testament ministry not according to the letter but according to the Spirit. The letter kills, but the Spirit gives life (2 Cor. 3:6). Therefore, when we go out, we need not only the word but also the Spirit. To have only the Spirit but not the word is abstract and empty. We need to have the word as the reality and content in order to supply life to others and cause them to grow in life. We need both the Spirit and the word. Although the Lord has led us to compile some concise, practical, and useful materials for the perfecting of the home meetings, we cannot depend wholly on such materials. What we rely on are the Spirit of God and the word of God. Concerning the Spirit of God, we must be rich in experience and knowledge and have much reserve. Concerning the word of God, we must enter into its depth and be saturated and equipped with it. In this way, we will be those who are filled with the Spirit of God and the word of God.

If someone is a person who is filled with the Spirit and the word of God, then wherever he goes and whomever he meets, as soon as he speaks to people, the spirit will come out, and they will receive life. At the same time, the word will also come out, and life will be ministered to them. The result is that people are enlivened and enabled to grow. If we can be such persons, our visiting new believers' homes every week for fifty-two weeks a year to perfect their home meetings will have a great impact. However, if we lack these two items, no matter how good our materials and methods are, we will be giving others only doctrines and letters. We will not be ministering life to enliven them or to enable them to grow. We should bear in mind that it is the Spirit of God and the word of God that can enliven others and cause them to grow.

The Word Being the Spirit and the Spirit Being the Word

The Bible is truly wonderful. Through our experience, we eventually realize that the word is the Spirit, and the Spirit is the word; the two are simply one. The Lord Jesus Himself once testified, "The words which I have spoken to you are spirit and are life" (John 6:63). The word is life, and the word is the Spirit. Initially, we experience only that the word is life. However, Ephesians 6:17 says, "The sword of the Spirit, which Spirit is the word of God." Those who know Greek understand that *word* refers not to *sword* but to *Spirit*. It is not that the word is the sword, but that the word as the sword is the Spirit. Thus, this verse reveals to us clearly that the word has become the Spirit, and the Spirit is the word.

If we are those who are filled with the Spirit of the Lord and the word of the Lord, then when we go out to contact people, what we speak to them will be the word, but when this word is received into them, it will become spirit and life.

What the Lord Jesus speaks to us is His word, but when this word enters into our being, it becomes spirit and life. Hence, the words which He has spoken to us are spirit and are life. Because the words we speak come from the Spirit, these words become spirit when they enter into people. Then when the spirit comes from them, it becomes word, and when this word enters into others, it again becomes spirit. This shows that in order to be useful in God's hands we must have the word and the Spirit, the Spirit and the word. What we hear is the word, but what we receive into us is the Spirit. Then what we speak forth is the word, but what others receive is the Spirit.

The word is the Spirit, and the Spirit is the word; the two are one. It is the Spirit who gives life (John 6:63). To give life means to enliven someone and to cause him to grow. Someone may have a dead spirit, but when we open our mouth to supply the Spirit to him, he is enlivened. This is to give him life. Someone else may be enlivened in his spirit, but he may lack the supply and not have enough life. When we supply him with the word, this word brings with it life that enters into him to supply him. The result is that he grows in life. First Peter 2:2 says, "Long for the guileless milk of the word in order that by it you may grow unto salvation." The milk of the word enables people to grow in life. We all know that whatever food we consume—whether it is milk, bread, meat, vegetables, or fruit—is able to supply us life and cause us to grow. That is why a small child who weighs only a few pounds at birth will weigh over a hundred pounds after a number of years. Growth altogether hinges on eating.

The Spirit gives life and enlivens; the word supplies life and causes the growth in life. It is by the word and the Spirit that we can perfect others.

(A message given on March 19, 1987 in Taipei, Taiwan)

CHAPTER ELEVEN

HOME MEETINGS
AND THE USE OF *LIFE LESSONS*

(1)

In order to perfect the home meetings, we should first learn to teach people how to sing hymns. In *Life Lessons,* which was compiled for the perfecting of the home meetings, a suitable hymn is included in each lesson. When we go to the home meetings, the first thing we should do is to teach the attendants to sing those hymns.

THE RHYME AND RHYTHM OF HYMNS

Some among us may be willing to bear the burden to compose some new hymns. This is very good. For this, we should have some basic knowledge about hymns. First, we need to know about the rhyme of hymns. To maintain a proper rhyme, the long lines have to rhyme with the long ones and the short lines with the short. In some hymns, the first line can rhyme with the second, while in other hymns this is not possible. Sometimes the first line has to rhyme with the third, and the second with the fourth. We need to pay much attention to this because the initial emphasis of a hymn lies in its rhyme. Chinese poetry is very concerned with the four phonetic tones. However, when a long poem is put to a tune, there should not be such a concern for tones. Since a hymn is a poem for singing, we do not need to care for the tones. As long as the words with the four tones are rhymed, it will be fine.

Another concern for the hymns is rhythm. The tempo and rhythm should correspond with each other. Putting lyrics to a tune is based on these two considerations. The rhythm of

Chinese poems is according to the Chinese writing style. For example, a ten-syllable sentence pattern can be in the combination of five and five or of four and six. The four-six pattern can be changed to six and four or five groups of two. These are all patterns that fit a ten-syllable sentence. Four and six, six and four, and five groups of two are all even-numbered patterns. However, the pattern of five and five is odd, so it cannot be put together with one of the even-numbered patterns. For example, in the Chinese supplemental hymnal, the first line of stanza 1 of hymn #835 reads, "What mercy that my eyes have seen the true God!" This sentence consists of eleven syllables arranged in a four-seven pattern. "What mercy that my eyes have seen" is four groups of two syllables, and the sentence ends with another three syllables. The following line of the hymn says, "What grace that I can freely have salvation!" This perfectly matches the pattern of the first sentence. Such a hymn is rhythmic and pleasant to our ears. This demonstrates that a hymn must have a proper rhythm.

With these points in mind, we will not compose hymns with strange combinations of mismatched rhythm, such as putting a three-five pattern together with a four-four pattern. *Hymns,* #1080 is one that has a good rhythm. Stanza 1 reads, "What profit all the labor here? / There's nothing new for you and me! / Remember not the former things, / They're all vanity!" These lines are in a three-five pattern in Chinese, and the tune and rhythm are well-matched. The last stanza says, "Remember God in days of youth! / Fear Him, and such will be your gain! / With Him you will be satisfied, / For He is not vain!" Although the first three lines are composed of eight syllables, in Chinese they all are in the pattern of three and five, not four and four. This provides a consistency in the rhythm.

BEING STEADFAST IN DOOR-KNOCKING
AND HOME MEETINGS

If you are the one out of every four saints who is willing to go door-knocking and visiting, you should consecrate the Lord's Day to the Lord. Then during the week you should offer three evenings. Since you have "joined the army," you should set aside your time; otherwise, you should not join.

The three evenings during the week all have different purposes. The first evening is to be trained in how to knock on doors, lead a home meeting, and use and teach from *Life Lessons*. Then having learned this, you should set aside two evenings to go out. One and a half evenings should be devoted to leading home meetings, and the remaining half evening should be used for door-knocking. You should not do too much door-knocking. We may compare this to having children. If you give birth to too many children, you will not be able to raise them. However, you should not stop begetting; you should continue to beget, but you should raise up the ones whom you have begotten. After two or three years you can beget two more and raise them gradually. In this way, life will propagate continuously. Never practice this out of a momentary excitement. Do not act only when you feel like doing it and then become cold when the excitement subsides. This is not the way. You must be steadfast until the Lord comes.

LEARNING TO WORK WITHOUT OPINIONS

In all our service we need to learn to have no opinions. Those who like to talk a lot and have many opinions often do not work much. Those who truly work do not talk much and do not have opinions. The capable ones among the co-workers usually do not have opinions. They simply do whatever is fellowshipped. The quiet ones are usually the ones who work; the talkative people are usually the ones who do not. We may illustrate this with the printing of *Life Lessons*. The last word was completed recently on a Friday at 9:05 P.M. Then the serving sisters immediately started working. Those who typed did the typing, and those who proofread did the proofreading. They worked until 2:00 A.M. because the manuscript had to be ready by Saturday morning for imaging, typesetting, and printing so the book could be ready by the coming Monday. That was a good coordination. The serving sisters did not say anything. Every one of them worked silently and diligently without any opinions. They worked entirely according to the instructions. Especially in proofreading, the sisters paid much attention to the use and choice of diction in the manuscript that I gave them. They all worked according to instructions without any opinions.

In theory, "every road leads to Rome"; there is not only one way. However, if everyone has something to say, and if everyone has his opinions, it will never be possible to "get to Rome." In American culture, the one who drives the car is properly respected. The one with the steering wheel in his hands is the one who drives, and everyone else in the car should not talk. This makes it very easy to get to the destination. If someone keeps giving opinions and argues, this will only waste time. Therefore, we should learn to work without opinions. Even if we know that the directions are not quite right, the "steering wheel" is not in our hands, so we should still remain silent. In this way, even though we may end up taking a few more turns, we quietly follow the "driver." Then we experience that all things are under the Lord's sovereign hands. He never fails us.

The capable ones do not talk much, while those who give opinions do not work much. This is an unchanging principle. Those who work know that there are different ways to do things, so it is not necessary to insist on a certain way, and there is no need to spend much time to study how to do things. For example, if we want to go to Yang-ming Shan, some may sit down to discuss which way is the shortest. As a result, they will discuss for over half an hour before they set out. Those who work faithfully will drive there right away and arrive in ten minutes, or twenty minutes at the most. What we need is only to "drive the car" and get there. From the beginning, the many young full-time serving ones among us need to learn the lesson of having no opinions and not giving any opinions. This is the proper attitude.

THE LEARNING NEEDED AND THE SUCCESS IN LEADING A HOME MEETING

To perfect a home meeting, the first thing we need to learn is to sing the hymns. We ourselves must be familiar with the tune of a hymn and sing it well before we can lead others to sing. If there are children in the homes, we need to encourage them to sing with us because children are the fastest learners of hymns. Upon hearing the hymns, the children will start humming them, and they will pick them up very quickly. They are truly the ones whom we can count on to start singing and lead the singing at home. Once they have learned the hymns, they can lead others to sing together. It is not very easy for older people to learn to sing hymns. Therefore, when we lead a home meeting, we need to encourage the children to sing and ask them to lead the singing. This is very needful.

Although *Life Lessons* has its own sequence of lessons, we do not need to be rigid about the sequence when we use the book. We can choose any one of the topics from it. The principle is that the choice should be based on our knowledge of the particular home and their practical needs. However, there are some lessons, like "Knowing the Church," which we must teach them. I believe that all of us who are leading a home meeting feel the need to teach this lesson. Basically, we need to learn every lesson well.

In order to use *Life Lessons* appropriately, we need to know the way the book is compiled. First, the Scripture reading in each lesson is very rich. The Scripture as the basis is the most outstanding feature and the richest part of the book. Second, the explanation of the Scripture is very simple. It is better to be simple. Because it is simple, it is easy for the new ones to understand, but it still has a crucial meaning and certain main points. Before we go to lead a home meeting, it is better for us to study one or two lessons. We not only need to study the verses thoroughly, but we also need to understand the main points in the explanation. In this way we can understand the book thoroughly. Moreover, no lesson exceeds six pages. Some lessons have only three pages. On average, each one is four to five pages. The portion is just right. At the end of each lesson there is a hymn. This is the summary of the whole compilation. It is best for us to follow this line when using the book.

CONSTANTLY SEEKING TO BE FILLED
WITH THE HOLY SPIRIT

The one who leads the meeting must be living. If he is not living, the meeting will definitely have no vitality. If we are a burning person, once we enter the meeting, everyone will be burning. If five or six people are together talking and laughing excitedly and someone comes in weeping, they will hardly be able to continue laughing. After a while others may begin to shed tears. This illustrates that one person's situation can greatly affect the meeting. If we are a weeping person yet try to give a message to make people laugh, no one will laugh. On the other hand, if we are a laughing person, yet we try to give a message on repentance, confession, fasting, mourning, and lamenting, we can shout at the top of our voice, but no one will cry or feel sorrowful.

In this matter we cannot pretend. If we pretend, we will just be performing like actors. We are not actors, so we should not act. Even if we act well, it will still be false. We should not put on a mask, let alone give a performance. Whether or not the leading ones are living depends on their daily living. If we walk according to the truth and the Spirit in our daily life, as time goes by we will be a certain kind of person. Then when we are in the home meetings, we will be those who walk according to the truth and the Spirit. Whether or not we speak, we will be such persons. The kind of living a person has is the kind of person he will be.

A person who is filled with the Spirit will bring the Spirit wherever he goes. When he speaks, the Spirit will come out. When he cries, the Spirit comes out, and when he laughs, the Spirit also comes out. When he reads the Bible, the Spirit comes out, and when he sings, the Spirit also comes out. This is the most important matter.

TRAINING OUR CHARACTER

We also need to train our character in our daily life. We not only seek the constant filling of the Holy Spirit, but we also need to have a good training of our character. Please consider the bookshelves of hymnals and Bibles for public use in various meeting halls. Are the books torn or falling apart? This kind of condition is not appropriate, and this tells us that we do not have a good character. We should know that when a proper person attends a Christian meeting, he will more or less pay attention to the clothing, speech, and behavior of the Christians and the setting of the meeting hall. We need to give people a grave, neat, proper, and dignified impression. All these are related to our spiritual character.

I was trained in my character since childhood. When I came home, I would arrange my shoes properly. I would return things to their original places after using them. Several days ago someone called me in Taipei from Anaheim. I was able to tell them clearly what I put in the right bottom drawer of the desk in my study and what I put in the second drawer on the left of the mirror in my bedroom. I asked them to bring me those things, and they made no mistake. I am an old man of eighty years of age. I say this in hope that the young people among us will train their character when they are young.

Character is cultivated. Man's character is a matter first of inward nature and second of outward expression. In 1953 I spoke about thirty-two items related to character. At that time I emphasized to the trainees that character is the development of our inborn nature and our acquired habits. While thirty percent of our character is our inborn nature, seventy percent is our acquired habits. Therefore, we all need to learn to be proper people, not only when we visit others in their home but also in our daily life. We should not be loose most of the time and then put on a performance when it is needed. We must continually build up our character in our daily living and seek to always be filled by the Holy Spirit. In this way we will succeed in leading the home meetings.

Currently we have about seven thousand new ones under our care, and there are still about ten thousand new ones whom we are not able to care for, mainly because we do not have enough people to take care of them. I tell you this in order to show you that whether or not the new way will succeed depends completely on the home meetings. If the home meetings are good, the new way will succeed, but if the home meetings are not good, the new way will fail. We believe that in some places the new way will be very successful, while in other places it will not succeed. In yet other places, the new way will half succeed and half fail. It all depends on how the elders and co-workers lead the church in their locality. The key is that they must lead the church in a proper way in order to succeed.

It is difficult for the trainees to live with several hundred people, let alone be trained twenty-four hours a day. However, this is to train their character and help them to exercise their spirit in order to adapt to the environment. Perhaps some of them are the only son or daughter at home, and they were spoiled by their parents and allowed to do whatever they liked. Today, however, since they have chosen to serve the Lord full-time, they must know that in serving the Lord there is not a single thing that will go according to their will. They must be prepared to have a mind to suffer.

A person who is as fragile as an egg cannot serve the Lord. Every person who serves the Lord must be like an egg of marble, even of steel that can withstand a nuclear attack. Only such a strong person can serve the Lord. If we hear a word that wrongs us or does not please us and become hurt and disappointed, then we will not be welcome anywhere. Therefore, we need to learn to be strong in our spirit within and meek without in order to adapt to every environment. This is to have a proper character. If people arrange that we sleep in a room by ourselves, we will be fine. If the arrangement is that we share a room with another person, even with two or three people, we are still fine. If we have to get up early, we are fine, and if we have to get up late, we are also fine. We should be adaptable in all things, whether tough or soft, square or round. Then we will be useful in the hands of the Lord.

AN EXAMPLE OF USING *LIFE LESSONS,*
LESSON TWELVE, ON "KNOWING THE CHURCH"

In using *Life Lessons* during a home meeting, we need to remember not to speak too much about other things. It is not even necessary to bring up other Bible verses because all the necessary verses are contained in the lesson. We need to share only what is in the lesson. Some of the contents do not require much time to read. The remaining time should be used to practice singing hymns with the new ones, and at the end we can have a little more time of fellowship with them.

When we read, we should read section by section. For example, the introduction of lesson twelve, "Knowing the Church," says, "The church is the goal God wants to obtain in His eternal economy." We should not read this rigidly. Since God's eternal economy is a major point, we need to read this several times and in a living way. For example, we can say, "Lord, thank You that the church is the goal God wants to obtain in His eternal economy. This is the goal which God plans to obtain in His eternal economy. Every saved person has a part in this goal. Thank You, Lord, we all have a part in God's eternal purpose." Lead everyone to read together, not just one person reading. This is the main thing to do. At the same time do not expect to explain the lesson thoroughly the first time. We need to learn that if we cannot explain the lesson thoroughly, we should leave the questions temporarily. Do not attempt to solve them. The new ones will gradually understand.

We must learn to lead the new ones to livingly read concerning the five basic items that Christians must know: first, to know the true God; second, to know Christ; third, to know the Holy Spirit; fourth, to know the cross of Christ; and fifth, to know the church. Every Christian must be completely familiar with these five points. In knowing the church, we first need to know that the church is the called-out assembly. Second, the church is the Body of Christ. Third, the church is the counterpart of Christ. Fourth, the church is the house of God. Fifth, the church is the new man. Then we need to explain that the first title, "the called-out assembly," is a general term. Then to Christ, the church is His Body and His counterpart, and to God, the church is His house. Finally, for the fulfillment of God's will, the church is a new man. By leading the new ones to read and speak in this way, it will be easy for them to remember the five main aspects of the church.

Next we need to come back to read section by section. For example, in the section on the Body of Christ, Ephesians 1:22b-23 says, "The church, which is His Body, the fullness of the One who fills all in all." The content of this section says, "The church is...constituted for Christ in His life and Spirit with all those who have believed into Him." Such a phrase as *in His life and Spirit* is an important point, and we need to read it a few more times. *Life Lessons* is written in a concise way. Every phrase is like a gold nugget that requires repeat-reading with emphasis. *Constituted for Christ* means not for others but for Christ. Furthermore, the church is constituted not by organization or coincidence but with life; therefore, it says "in His life." It is also constituted with Spirit, so it says "and Spirit."

We should not read this passage too fast. All the important points need to be read repeatedly. Sometimes we need to read loudly or even proclaim, but sometimes we may need to read softly. We should practice this kind of reading privately and not wait until we come to the home meeting. To practice repeat-reading is to read over and over again. We also need to practice reading loudly, softly, slowly, quickly, and in a proclaiming way. The lesson itself already gives a clear explanation, so it is not necessary to speak more. It is sufficient simply to read in various ways to express it. Some of the sentences in particular cannot be explained and should not be explained. Once you attempt to explain them, you will deviate from the right meaning. We only need to read them as they are.

The way a child learns to speak is wonderful. For example, when he learns to say "water glass," he may not fully understand what water is and what a glass is, but he understands "water glass." Perhaps he once pointed to a water glass and asked what it was. After people said "water glass" a few times, he learned it. It would be redundant to explain that water is a fluid and that a glass is for containing things, and this kind of explanation might confuse the child. We only need to teach him to repeat "water glass" after us a few times, and he will learn. Therefore, do not overly elaborate. I believe that this example will help you understand and receive the benefit.

When we first start reading with the newly saved ones, they may feel they do not know what they are reading. Nevertheless, simply lead them to read a few times. You do not need to say too much. It is enough to say only a little, and they will understand. This lesson can be used for twenty minutes, fifty minutes, or even an hour. The speaking of twenty minutes has its benefits; the speaking of fifty minutes has its benefits; and the speaking of one hour has its benefits. The more closely we follow the lesson, the more they can understand. Do not speak anything other than the words from the lessons and the Bible. I hope that we can all see that this is the way to constitute God's truth into people. If we do this every week for fifty-two weeks a year, we can expect a result.

THE PROSPECT OF THE SUCCESS OF THE NEW WAY

This step is the high mountain of the new way, and we must climb it in one accord. If the home meeting is successful, the blessing of the Lord will be with us.

At the present time we have more than ten thousand saints meeting in the church in Taipei. There are more than three thousand saints meeting in twenty-three meeting halls and more than seven thousand saints meeting in thousands of homes. In the coming years, we hope that there will be more than one hundred thousand saints meeting regularly in Taipei. How glorious it would be to have this many saints meeting on a single Lord's Day. Whether or not the new way will be successful is a matter of God's eternal purpose, and it depends on whether or not we are willing to do it. The problem today lies not with the way but with whether or not we are willing to take this way and how we take it. I hope that we would all have the same feeling and be in one accord, willing to put our shoulders to the task and take this new way, which is ordained by God.

On the other hand, we still need big meetings. If the Lord has mercy on us, He will allow us to build a big meeting hall in Taipei which can accommodate fifteen to seventeen thousand people so that we can blend with one another.

In any case, we must take this new way. Whether or not this way will be successful depends very much on the trainees. When they go back to their own localities, they should spread the new way and become teachers to train the saints in every place. In this way, after five years this will become our "family tradition." Then it will not be as difficult as it is today. We may compare this to the way education has been made universal in Taiwan. Because a complete educational system has been established, it is easy to make education universal. We should do something of the same kind. We should work out the crucial points so that the new way can be universalized. Once the new way is universalized, the result will be amazing. Then in a few years hundreds and thousands, even tens of thousands, of saints in Taiwan will go to many places to gospelize the world.

Five hundred thousand saints in Taipei can produce twenty-five thousand full-timers. Since Taiwan does not need this many, these full-timers can go to the whole world. They can go to the Arab nations, India, South Africa, East Africa, and West Africa. Some can go even to northern Europe. If possible, one day we will send some to Russia to gospelize the people there. This is our prospect. We must believe that this will work. Moreover, if the one hundred thousand saints who regularly meet are faithful with regard to their income and consecration to make financial offerings, the supply for the full-timers should be more than adequate.

Finally, we need to declare that this is the proper way. When this way starts flowing, it will be not only a few drops of water but a flood. We all must press forward to succeed in the home meetings, to gospelize Taiwan, and to gospelize the whole world. This is too glorious!

(A message given on March 24, 1987 in Taipei, Taiwan)

CHAPTER TWELVE

HOME MEETINGS
AND THE USE OF *LIFE LESSONS*

(2)

SOME FELLOWSHIP REGARDING HYMNS

Our Chinese hymnal has approximately eight hundred hymns. Even though some of the hymns were selected from outside sources, none of them were simply copied exactly or compiled without being revised. Some originally were old English hymns that were spread to China one or two hundred years ago and translated into Chinese. When we adopted these hymns, we revised and edited all of them.

Among the collection of old hymns there were certainly some good ones, but even in these good hymns some of the wording was not according to the truth. For example, one hymn says, "In tenderness He sought me, / Weary and sick with sin, / And on His shoulders brought me / Into His flock again" (English *Hymns,* #1068). The original hymn speaks of being led back to His "fold," which is not according to the Bible. The fold refers to Judaism as a religious organization. In John 10 the Lord said that He would lead His sheep out of the fold. He also said that there were other sheep which were not of this fold; He would lead them both and they would become one flock (v. 16). The fold is where the sheep are kept temporarily on winter nights, which signify times of trouble. Therefore, the fold is the product of abnormal times. However, the writers of the hymns in Christianity regard the fold as a pleasant thing. This was contradictory to the truth. The Lord Jesus leads people out from the fold, but the hymn writers have opened the fold wide again and called the sheep back in.

A century ago hymns written in English often ended with something related to the "heavenly mansion." One of these hymns is based on the historical fact of the Israelites' crossing the Jordan River and entering into the land of Canaan. Canaan is considered the heavenly mansion and the Jordan as the river of death. There are frequent references to things such as this. Therefore, although an original hymn was actually good, we still revised it, even if only one of the stanzas or a few of the sentences were not according to the truth. In our English hymnal every word and sentence of the eight hundred hymns we use were considered diligently. Afterward, the Chinese hymns were composed based on the English hymns.

AN ILLUSTRATION OF THE USE OF *LIFE LESSONS*

Lesson eleven of *Life Lessons* is entitled "Knowing the Cross of Christ." It begins by speaking of "the cross of Christ...according to the requirements of God's righteousness, holiness, and glory." Here are three sources of requirements: righteousness, holiness, and glory. The Lord has fulfilled all these so that He "accomplished God's eternal redemption for us...to become the basis of our eternal salvation." Here we see both redemption and salvation. Salvation is different from redemption. Redemption was accomplished on the cross, while salvation is the application of the redemption of the cross to us. We receive redemption, and redemption becomes salvation to us. Therefore, redemption is objective and was accomplished on the cross, whereas salvation is subjective and is applicable to us. These are the things that we need to know.

The Cross Being Prophesied by God

First, we need to know that the cross was prophesied by God. Christ has redeemed us out of the curse of the law, having become a curse on our behalf (Gal. 3:13). In verse 13 the Scripture says that Christ has become a curse on our behalf, but the Chinese Union Version says that Christ was cursed on our behalf. We need to see that Christ not only was cursed, but He actually became a curse on our behalf to redeem us out of the curse of the law. In Genesis 3 the first thing that happened to man after the fall was that he was cursed.

Because of man's fall sin came in; therefore, all of fallen mankind is under God's curse. Thank Him, the Savior Christ came to fallen mankind, and having been born under law and being under the law, He became a curse on our behalf to bear our curse so that we would be redeemed out of the curse of the law. As it is written, "Cursed is everyone hanging on a tree" (Gal. 3:13). In this way we can see that the cross was prophesied by God.

The Old Testament also prophesied that crucifixion was not an ordinary punishment or execution but an extraordinary one. In the Old Testament there is a prophecy that uses the phrase "hang...on a tree" (Deut. 21:22). Therefore, when the apostle Peter spoke of the crucifixion of Christ in 1 Peter 2:24, he used a similar phrase: "Who Himself bore up our sins in His body on the tree." Galatians 3:13 also says, "Cursed is everyone hanging on a tree." In the Old Testament the cross was prophesied at an early time, in Deuteronomy 21:22-23. The tree here refers to the cross that was made out of wood. In Deuteronomy the ordinance of the law which God established with man explicitly speaks of a man being cursed by hanging on a tree. As a result, the words in that ordinance became a prophecy, prophesying that Christ would hang on a tree, that is, be crucified on the cross.

The Cross Being a Roman Form of Execution

Second, we should know that crucifixion was a Roman form of execution. The Jews cried to Pilate, saying, "Take Him away! Take Him away! Crucify Him!" Then Pilate, the Roman governor, said to them, "Shall I crucify your King?" The chief priests answered, "We have no king except Caesar," the ruler of the Roman Empire (John 19:15). This shows us that the punishment of crucifixion was a Roman form of execution. The Jewish form of execution was to stone a criminal to death (Deut. 22:24). However, about sixty years before the Lord's birth, the Jewish nation fell to Rome. Not long before the Lord was put to death by the Roman governor, the Roman Empire had adopted crucifixion from other nations as the form of execution for the most evil persons.

Thus, when the Jews sought to kill the Lord, they crucified

Him through the hands of the Roman governor, fulfilling God's prophecy in Deuteronomy 21:23 concerning how the Lord would die. This was done by the sovereign hand of God. If the Roman Empire had not adopted crucifixion, or if the Jewish nation had not fallen to the control of the Roman Empire, or if the Romans had destroyed the Jewish nation, then the crucifixion of the Lord Jesus could not have taken place. This shows us the sovereign hand of God—to allow the Jewish nation to fall to Rome and to cause the Roman Empire to adopt crucifixion as the form of execution at that time. These were all for the preparation of the Lord's death.

The Time When Christ Was Crucified

Furthermore, we should also know the time when Christ was crucified. Christ was crucified beginning at nine o'clock in the morning: "Now from the sixth hour darkness fell over all the land until the ninth hour" (Matt. 27:45). The situation of the universe changed because the age had changed. From nine o'clock to noon was one period of time, and from noon to three o'clock in the afternoon was another period. Between these two periods, darkness fell over the heaven and the earth. In other words, God came in to deal with sin by causing Christ to bear all the sins of man.

Christ was crucified for a total of six hours, from nine o'clock in the morning to three o'clock in the afternoon. In the first three hours, it was men who persecuted Him; it was not yet God who punished Him on behalf of us sinners. In these three hours He suffered in martyrdom and not yet for redemption. We need to be clear about this. The first three hours of suffering were for the sake of the truth, in martyrdom, not for redemption. Then at noon the whole earth became dark. From this time until three o'clock, God came to judge Christ in the sinners' place. According to Isaiah 53, God put our sins on Him (v. 6). In these three hours God judged us sinners and our sins by judging the Lord Jesus. This was not a continuation of men's persecution of Him. In these three hours He suffered for redemption, not in martyrdom.

Of the same period of punishment on the cross, the first half was in martyrdom, while the second half was in redemption. In the first half, men persecuted Him. At noon darkness fell over the heaven and the earth, and God placed our sins on the Lord Jesus Christ. At that time the hands of men stopped, and God came in to judge Him. During this time the Lord cried, "My God, My God, why have You forsaken Me?" (Matt. 27:46) The only answer is, "For the sins of us sinners."

The Accomplishments of the Cross

Next, we need to know the accomplishments of the cross. First, 1 Peter 2:24 says, "Who Himself bore up our sins [plural, referring to man's sins in his outward deeds] in His body on the tree, in order that we, having died to sins, might live to righteousness." The first thing Christ accomplished on the cross was to bear the various sins in our outward behavior, that is, our "personal sins." *Personal sins* is a term in Chinese theology which is not commonly found elsewhere. The "personal sins" are the sins committed by man personally. Christ bore our sins on the cross so that we may be saved, passing out of death into life.

Second, Hebrews 9:26 says, "But now...for the putting away of sin [singular, referring to man's sin in his inward nature] through the sacrifice of Himself." *Sins* (plural) refers to man's sins in his outward deeds, while *sin* (singular) is man's sin in his inward nature. On the cross the second thing that Christ did was to remove the sin in our inward nature, that is, the sin inherited by birth. This "original sin" was inherited from Adam, who sinned and passed it on to us. One kind of sin is the "personal sin," and the other is the "original sin," the inherited sin. Through sacrificing Himself on the cross, Christ also freed us from the inward, sinful nature. Therefore, the Lord Jesus dealt with the two aspects of sin on the cross. On the one hand, He bore our many sins, which are the sins in our outward deeds, and on the other hand, He also bore our inward, singular sin, which is the sin in our nature.

Third, Galatians 3:13 says, "Christ has redeemed us out of the curse of the law, having become a curse on our behalf; because...'Cursed is everyone hanging on a tree.'" Christ bore our outward sins and removed our inward sin on the cross, receiving the curse which, according to God's law, we should have received because of our fall and our sin.

Fourth, Romans 6:6 says, "Knowing this, that our old man has been crucified with Him in order that the body of sin might be annulled, that we should no longer serve sin as slaves." Christ has crucified our old man on the cross, and once our old man died, the body was made of none effect. When a man dies, his body is made of none effect. Those who smoke opium cannot quit no matter how hard they try because there is an addiction within their bodies. However, once a person dies, his body, having been annulled and made of none effect, can no longer smoke opium. Our old man has been crucified with the Lord Jesus so that our body of sin may be made of none effect, so that we should no longer be slaves to sin. Therefore, Christ not only dealt with our twofold sin on the cross—the personal sins in our outward deeds and the inherited sin in our inward nature—but even more, He crucified our sinful old man that the body of sin might be made of none effect, that we should no longer be slaves to sin.

Fifth, Galatians 2:20 says, "I am crucified with Christ." "I" is our old man. *Old man* and *I* refer to the same thing. Since our old man has been crucified with Christ, our "I" is also crucified with Him.

Sixth, 5:24 says, "But they who are of Christ Jesus have crucified the flesh with its passions and its lusts." Not only did Christ crucify our old man on the cross; He also crucified our flesh with its passions and lusts. Here it says that we who are of Christ have crucified the flesh with the passions and the lusts. We can do this based on what the Lord accomplished on the cross in crucifying our flesh. We can now apply to us that fact that was accomplished by the Lord.

Seventh, Hebrews 2:14-15 says, "...blood and flesh, He [Christ] also Himself in like manner partook of the same, that through death He might destroy him who has the might of death, that is, the devil, and might release those who because of the fear of death through all their life were held in slavery." Because of the fear of death, men were held in slavery and thus became slaves of death. On the cross Christ destroyed the devil, who has the might of death, and released us from the slavery of death.

Eighth, John 3:14-15 says, "And as Moses lifted up the serpent [on a pole] in the wilderness...." This is a second prophecy in the Old Testament. In the Old Testament the bronze serpent was lifted up on a pole, and in the New Testament, "...so must the Son of Man be lifted up [on the cross], that everyone who believes into Him may have eternal life." Since on the cross Christ destroyed the devil, who has the might of death, He also judged and dealt with the old serpent who had poisoned mankind, that all who believe in Christ may have God's eternal life and pass from death into life. This is typified by Moses' lifting up the serpent in the wilderness, which brought the Israelites out of death into life.

Ninth, Galatians 6:14 says, "Through whom [Christ] the world has been crucified to me." On the cross Christ destroyed Satan the devil, and at the same time He crucified the world organized by Satan and hanging on Satan, causing the world to lose its usurping power on those who have believed into Christ.

Tenth, Ephesians 2:14-15 says, "For He Himself [Christ]... has made both [the Jews and the Gentiles] one and has broken down the middle wall of partition, the enmity, abolishing in His flesh the law of the commandments in ordinances, that He might create the two in Himself into one new man, so making peace." On the cross Christ abolished the Old Testament law of the commandments in ordinances, which separated the Jews from the Gentiles, making them one and creating the two in Himself into one new man, which is the church.

Eleventh, John 12:24 says, "Unless the grain of wheat [typifying Christ] falls into the ground and dies, it abides alone; but if it dies, it bears much fruit [typifying the members of Christ]." Christ not only dealt with all the above negative items for God and for us on the cross, but through His death on the cross He also released the divine life from within Him into us so that we could become His many members, which constitute His Body.

The above total to eleven major items. The first ten items are negative, while the last item is positive. The first ten items kill and abolish, while the last item releases life and dispenses life into us so that we can be His living members.

Boasting in the Cross

Lastly, we need to boast in the cross. Galatians 6:14 says, "But far be it from me to boast except in the cross of our Lord Jesus Christ." Those zealous for the Jewish religion forced others to be circumcised in order to boast in others' flesh (vv. 12-13). However, the apostle Paul, being gained by Christ, did not boast in anything but the cross of Christ.

AN ADDITIONAL WORD OF FELLOWSHIP

When leading the home meetings, we must remember to do away with tradition, ordinances, rituals, and religion, including reading the Bible and praying in a religious way. However, do not eliminate these things too quickly. If there is a new friend in the home, first introduce him to everyone in a normal way. Do not be short of a human touch, as if you cannot be a human when you take away tradition and religion. This is unnatural and inappropriate. We should introduce new ones or family members among us in a normal and informal way for everyone to become acquainted with each other. We need to contact people in a normal way.

We are often lacking in boldness. Therefore, we need to exercise and not panic. When we go to a new one's home, whether there are few or many, men or women, old or young, we should not be afraid and certainly not be cowardly. Our cowardice and timidity are bondages that Satan has put on us without our knowledge. We need to break through these. When we speak, we should conduct ourselves gracefully. Our voice should be loud and clear so that people can hear us. We also need to repeat-read, emphasize-read, and pray-read in a flexible way. This will make our meetings new and living.

We also need to see that reading is the most important matter. Good reading enlivens people, while bad reading kills people. We should adjust our voice to be high, low, fast, or slow according to what is appropriate. All this requires practice. A basketball player needs to practice his basic movements every day. The more he practices, the more skillful he becomes.

Then his movements will be very spontaneous and skillful when he is in a game.

I hope that once a person is saved he can use *Life Lessons*. However, this depends on the individual's condition. For those who are more seeking, we can give them more, perhaps two lessons every week or two meetings a week with two lessons each time. For others it might not be the same. There is no need to push or restrain people. Simply give them something according to their condition, and do not be rigid. Let those who are slow be slow. If we push them too much, they will not be able to digest what we give them, and they may even be stumbled. However, if we do not adequately feed those who are earnestly seeking and have a large capacity, they may become uneasy. We can compare this to a meal; if the food is suddenly taken away while we are still enjoying it, it is difficult to bear the dissatisfaction within. We need to lead them in a very flexible way, giving people whatever they need. This requires us to spend time in reading the content of the lessons thoroughly so we can apply it skillfully.

(A message given on March 26, 1987 in Taipei, Taiwan)

CHAPTER THIRTEEN

HOME MEETINGS
AND THE USE OF *LIFE LESSONS*

(3)

CONCERNING *LIFE LESSONS*

Since *Life Lessons* and the home meetings are closely related, we need to have a basic knowledge of *Life Lessons.*

Being Specifically for Use
in the Home Meetings of New Believers

First, the *Life Lessons* have been specifically prepared for the home meetings of new believers. The first two volumes cover different matters between a believer and God which he should know, understand, and practice immediately after his salvation. Then the last two volumes cover the full salvation which God has prepared in Christ for us who have believed into Him, the riches which we have obtained in Christ, the experience which we should have in Christ, the things which we should accomplish in Christ, and the goal which we should attain in Christ.

There Being No Need
for Added Explanation While Reading

Second, it is difficult to avoid certain terms which are relatively deep and hard for new believers to understand. There is no need for added explanation while reading these lessons in the meetings. As lesson after lesson is read, a thorough understanding of the terms will be acquired. Even if there is not such a thorough understanding at the time, this understanding will be gained gradually.

Only Christ Being Reality
and Only the Spirit Giving Life

Third, knowledge is empty and the letter kills; only Christ is reality and only the Spirit gives life. Thus, there must be prayer, confession of sins, and the abundantly rich filling and saturation with the Spirit of Christ before reading these lessons. In reading, there should be the practice of depending less on the mind and more on the spirit, rejecting the old way of knowledge and emphasizing the new way of life. Sentence after sentence that is being read should be pushed out by the spirit with life that others' spirits may be touched for them to receive the life supply of the pneumatic Christ. This point can be considered to be the most important.

As a matter of fact, the word of God does not require us to use our mind too much to think. Rather, it requires our spirit to touch the Holy Spirit. Then we are spontaneously enlightened within. Thinking causes us to have only knowledge, and knowledge is merely the letter, which is empty and which kills. When we use our spirit, we touch life. Life contains Christ, and Christ is the reality.

If we all exercise in this way when leading a home meeting, from the beginning people will touch the Spirit in their spirit, touching Christ and receiving life. They will not fall into Christianity's old way of knowledge. We have observed in certain students in the seminaries that the more they read the Bible, the more deadened they become. As they study, God seems to be gone, and their faith toward God is also gone. God is Spirit, and those who worship Him must worship Him in spirit and must use their spirit. If they use the wrong organ, they will have no way to worship God. If a person is speaking, but we cover our ears and only keep our eyes open, we will hear nothing. We hear with our ears, and we see with our eyes. In the same way, in order to touch God we must use our spirit.

The Bible is not merely the letter. The Bible is God's word, which is spirit and life. The Lord Jesus told His disciples, "The words which I have spoken to you are spirit and are life" (John 6:63). He said to the Jews that He is the bread of life and that he who eats Him shall live because of Him (vv. 48, 57).

However, they did not know how to use their spirit but could use only their mind. As a result, they could not understand Him and began a contention.

In John 5:39-40 the Lord Jesus said to the Jews, "You search the Scriptures, because you think that in them you have eternal life....Yet you are not willing to come to Me that you may have life." The Jews searched the Scriptures not only once; they searched them again and again. However, the Lord said, "Yet you are not willing to come to Me that you may have life." This shows us that we may search the Scriptures, but we may not necessarily receive life. If we merely read the Bible without coming forward to the Lord and drawing near to Him, we can receive only knowledge but not the Lord of life. Knowledge is empty, and the letter kills. Only Christ is reality, and only the Spirit gives life. Therefore, the Lord Jesus told the disciples, "The words which I have spoken to you are spirit and are life" (6:63).

Rejecting the Old Way of Knowledge and Emphasizing the New Way of Life

What is the old way of knowledge? We may illustrate this with John 1:1, which says, "In the beginning was the Word." If a person who reads this verse studies it only with his mind, he will ask what "in the beginning" is. When is "the beginning"? What does "the beginning" mean? As a result, he may go to check with the dictionary and discover that in Chinese there is only "in the ancient times" and not "in the beginning." We may use another example in which a person reads Genesis 1:1: "In the beginning God created the heavens and the earth." He may ask, "What is this God? How did He create the heavens and the earth?" As a result, after thinking for half a day, he still will not understand anything. This is the old way of knowledge, a natural and lifeless way of reading. A person may read the Bible for half a year or a full year and not receive any life at all.

It is this old way of knowledge that we have to reject. When we open the Bible, we should care for nothing else. The Bible says, "In the beginning," and we should follow to say, "In the beginning. Amen, in the beginning. Amen! Oh, the beginning

is the starting point. In the beginning was the Word. Amen!
Oh, at the starting point was the Word. Amen! The Word was
God. Praise the Lord, at the starting point was God! Oh, in
the beginning was God, and God is the starting point, the
origin, and the source!" If we read in this way, we will receive
life. We can use another example. Genesis 1:1 says, "In the
beginning God created the heavens and the earth." We may
pray, "Oh, God created. Praise the Lord, God did not form or
make the heavens and the earth, but He created them! Oh,
God created the heavens. God created the earth. Eventually,
He created me!" In this way the Bible, the word of God, is
applied to us. This is the proper way to read the Bible, reading it in the way of life.

Over thirty years ago we began to have a "life-study" of the
Bible. Previously such a thing could not be found in the history of Christianity. From that day onward, our study of the
Bible has been a study in life, not in knowledge. We study
with our spirit, not with our mind, and we study by prayer, not
by thinking. If we study by thinking, we would use our mind
to explain. This is the old way of knowledge. Instead, we study
with our spirit, which requires us to pray. What do we pray
with? We pray with the Scriptures that we read. For example,
in the sentence, "In the beginning God created the heavens
and the earth," there are five excellent words or phrases: "in
the beginning," "God," "created," "the heavens," and "the earth."
Although we do not read mainly with our mind, this does not
mean that we do not use our mind at all. We still have to
use our mind to understand the text. We need to understand
the literal meaning of this sentence—"in the beginning God
created the heavens and the earth"—by using our mind.
Therefore, when we read the Bible, we read with our eyes,
then comprehend with our mind, and then receive what we
read with our spirit.

Reading with the eyes, comprehending with the mind, and
receiving with the spirit are the three steps of reading the
Bible. A big mistake of the old way of knowledge in general is
that after people read with their eyes, they think too much
with their mind without going on to the third step of receiving

with their spirit. The ones who read in this way do not seem to have a spirit, or their spirit seems to be dead, so they rely entirely on their mind. Consequently, after studying for a long period of time, they are killed and do not receive any life supply. Whatever we do, we need to use the right organ. Therefore, when we read a verse like Genesis 1:1, we read first with our eyes, we understand the text with our mind, and then we receive and assimilate these words with our spirit. How do we use the spirit? It is by praying. We can compare this to walking. Can we forget about our legs and use our nose, ears, shoulders, or head to walk? We all would say that this is foolish. In order to walk we must use our legs. When we step out with our legs, we spontaneously are walking. It is the same with spiritual matters. Once we pray, we are using our spirit: "O Lord Jesus! In the beginning. Oh, in the beginning God! God created. Oh, God created the heavens, the earth, and man! God also created me. Thank You, God, You created the heavens and the earth, and You also created me." In this way our spirit is activated.

By Means of Much Prayer and Pray-reading, Causing Others to Receive the Life Supply

When we are sad, we should not try to listen to joyful messages. The more we listen to them, the sadder we may become. Neither should we use our mind to look for some verses in the Bible about rejoicing. We simply need to open up the Bible. When we read, "In the beginning God created the heavens and the earth," we can say to the Lord, "O Lord, in the beginning! O Lord! In the beginning! In the beginning God created." Once we use our spirit in this way to touch God, we will spontaneously rejoice. It is not by reading the word *rejoice* that we rejoice. Rather, we rejoice when we use the spirit to touch God. Similarly, some people say that Christians should have power, but we do not have power by talking about power. Instead, power comes from our touching God through pray-reading. This is a very wonderful matter.

In the past some people said that what we are saying here is merely a kind of psychology. They say that when a person calls on the Lord and pray-reads, he is only emotionally released and uplifted. If this is only psychological, they can try praying to George Washington, calling, "George! O George! O Washington!" He can also try calling on Confucius or a popular Chinese idol to see if he will receive an inner feeling. It is remarkable that the more a person calls on an idol or George Washington, the less of a joyful feeling he has. However, when he calls, "O Lord Jesus! O Lord Jesus!" the more joyful and powerful he feels within. This is absolutely not a matter of mental response, because calling other names has no effect. Only by our calling on the unique name of the Lord Jesus will something happen inwardly.

If pray-reading is entirely a matter of mental response, a person can also try to pray-read the newspaper and see what happens. For example, a newspaper headline may read, "Government decides to suspend foreign exchange controls." One can start to read aloud, "Oh, foreign exchange controls! Government suspended!" Consider what the result will be. However, if we open up the Bible, even only to Matthew 1 which contains the genealogy of Jesus Christ, we can pray-read, "Abraham begot Isaac, and Isaac begot Jacob, and Jacob begot Judah and his brothers." If we pray-read in this way, we will all be enlivened.

We all must realize that in order to use our spirit we have to pray. If we do not pray, we will have no way to use our spirit. It is impossible to use our spirit with our mouth shut and our eyes closed. Suppose I try to walk, but my two feet determine not to move. No matter how hard you command me to walk, it will be futile. As long as you use your spirit to pray, that is sufficient. It is not necessary to continually command ourselves to move our legs; as long as we walk, we are moving our legs. Similarly, it is not necessary to cry and shout in order to pray. Even if we speak to the Lord gently from within, "O Lord Jesus, O Lord Jesus, O Lord Jesus," our spirit will be activated. Once we pray, our spirit moves.

I hope that every time we lead a home meeting, we will do this. Then others will spontaneously follow. A mother teaches her child to speak not by reasoning but by speaking to him directly. When she says, "A rubber ball," the child says, "A rubber ball." When she says, "Play the ball," the child says, "Play the ball." When she says, "Kick the ball," the child says, "Kick the ball." As the child gradually understands, he will speak. Then when he grows older, he can speak everything. He will know how to say something even though no one has taught him to say it. This is very wonderful. Do not worry that you and other people do not understand the Bible. You simply need to pray and pray-read more and teach others to do the same. Then spontaneously and gradually they will understand.

We have to exercise to rely less on our mind and more on our spirit, rejecting the old way of knowledge and paying attention to the new way of life, by pushing out the word we read, sentence by sentence, by the spirit which brings life. Life is Christ, and Christ is in our spirit. When we use our spirit and push out our spirit, Christ is brought out. By using the spirit which brings life, we can push out the Spirit of God. Here we need to "push" and not merely to think. In this way we can touch others' spirit so that they may receive the pneumatic Christ as the life supply.

We need to learn this particularly when we read with others in the home meetings. We must exercise to depend less on the mind and more on our spirit, reading sentence after sentence. Not only should we read the words, but we also need to use our spirit and push out our spirit to turn the words into prayer, which will bring forth Christ. Then our spirit will touch others' spirit. When we use our spirit to read the Scriptures to others, this kind of reading will touch the spirit in them. This will affect them. We all need to learn to pray and read the Bible with our spirit to push out the word. The word entering into others will become the Spirit, which touches the spirit within them so that they can gain Christ in the spirit as the life supply. This is very important.

Needing to Repeat-read, Emphasize-read, Vitalize-read, and Pray-read

The Bible verses in *Life Lessons* may not be quoted in their entirety but only in part, economically according to the need. Therefore, the verses are quoted concisely, not too much or too little, and adequately, being most suitable for the new believers.

Furthermore, their explanations are both concise and adequate, having no need for further explanation. The only need is to repeat-read and emphasize-read. To repeat-read is to read with repetition, and to emphasize-read is to read with stress.

Besides repeat-reading and emphasize-reading, we also need to "vitalize-read." To vitalize-read is to do what we mentioned before in the example of Genesis 1:1. As we read this verse, we can give thanks to God, thanking Him for creating the heavens, the earth, you, and me. Reading in this way will vitalize us. This is to apply the word in a flexible way without diverging from the subject and main points. We have seen the need to repeat-read, emphasize-read, and vitalize-read. Now we also have to add pray-reading.

If we want to read the Bible in a living way, none of these four ways of reading can be omitted. For example, when we read a verse and find it very good, we can first repeat-read it, then emphasize-read it, then vitalize-read it, and then pray-read it. These four ways combined together form an effective method for reading. Pray-reading contains repeat-reading, emphasize-reading, and vitalize-reading. These four ways mingled together is the best reading method. This does not come merely from our thinking but from our experience.

In the home meetings, hymns are also indispensable. Hence, there is a hymn attached to every lesson. We need to learn to use the hymns in a flexible way and not to sing in a rigid way every time. For example, if a hymn has six stanzas, you do not need to sing all six stanzas. You may sing only the stanza that is suitable. If only the chorus is suitable, you can sing only the chorus. Sometimes you need to match the singing with a small testimony, not a lengthy one that will use up the time. Never extend the meaning of the text or develop an understanding based on inference. Never think that you are experienced. Once you extend and infer, you will easily be side-tracked from the subject and the central lane.

A FEW MATTERS CONCERNING THE HOME MEETINGS

The Bread-breaking Meeting

We need to fellowship about a few matters related to the

home meetings. We all know that the home meetings are the most important item of our present practice. We all must learn to exercise our spirit to touch people's condition and observe all the situations so that we can make the correct decisions concerning them.

Take the bread-breaking meeting for instance. We do not have a set rule about this meeting. For example, after leading the home meeting in a certain home for three to five times, or even ten to twenty times, we should set up a Lord's table meeting for them. We can compare this to studying; after we read a few lessons, we need to give them an advanced curriculum. If we do not first observe their situation, we should not make a decision concerning the Lord's table meeting. We must first study their condition, leading them in meeting after meeting. We should lead them to the point where we can sense that the inner condition of the few saved ones in this home is stable before the Lord. Furthermore, we must sense that there is nothing pertaining to idols in the furnishing and environment of this home and nothing that will cause damage to the Lord's testimony. When the condition of the home is ready, we can lead them to start breaking bread. In this way we have no set rule in this matter.

After this home has started to break the bread, it may reach the point where there is a need to bring in another two or three homes to break bread together. When this is appropriate depends on the condition of the home and our inner feeling. It is not possible to have a set rule.

The Offering of Material Riches

The offering of material riches is not a simple matter, and we also cannot make a set rule regarding this. There may be two or three or even many different ways of doing it. The first way is to come to the meeting hall to offer every Lord's Day. We hope that the brothers and sisters who meet regularly will take this way. However, a brother may have met in the same meeting hall for thirty years, always bringing an offering to the Lord when he comes to break bread, either on the Lord's Day morning or evening. Now that the church is taking the new way to meet, he will be burdened to meet in the home meetings, so he will not be able to come to the meeting in the meeting hall. However, if it is possible and if time allows, before he goes to the home meeting, he can go to the meeting hall to see the brothers and sisters and see what is happening there. At that time he can drop his offering in the offering box, and then he can go to the home meeting. This is a good way. On the one hand, we can meet in the small meetings in the homes, and on the other hand, we can also care for the big meeting in the meeting hall. It is very good if we can take care of both. This is the first way to make an offering.

The second way is to carefully and properly put out an offering box in the home where we meet. In order to do this, we should arrange for at least two persons, or better yet three, to serve together. It does not necessarily matter if they are brothers who serve in this way, or if they are sisters. They simply need to be honest and faithful, keeping a proper account and record whenever they open the offering box and count the offerings in it. In addition, in every Lord's table meeting there can be an offering box. As soon as the meeting ends, those who serve should open the offering box and not wait for another day. Then after these two or three brothers or sisters open the box and count and record the offerings, they should sign their names in an appropriate format.

Depending on the situation, the serving ones can decide how to hand over the offerings each week to the meeting hall where they meet. When the offerings are handed over, it is again necessary to have certain procedures, including a record of signatures that confirms the amount of the offerings and from which home meeting they were received.

Children's Meetings

The brothers and sisters who meet regularly in the homes may have been accustomed to meeting corporately in the meeting hall. When they went there, they brought their children so that while the adults were meeting, the children could also have their meeting at the same time. Now that some of these brothers and sisters attend the home meetings, the arrangement for their children will become a problem. Again, there is no fixed way. You should decide what to do according to the actual circumstances at that time. If certain home meetings are located near each other, the children can be grouped together to be cared for in one home. Alternatively, it is not bad to bring them to the home meeting to be blended with the children at that home. This requires us to observe the situation while we are carrying it out.

Leading Others to Know the Church

The last thing, which is also the most important thing, is that we should not keep people only in the home meetings and not let them contact the big meetings. This does not work. To do something in particular may not be necessary at the beginning, but gradually we have to bring them into the knowledge of the church. There are several ways to do this, so we need to be flexible.

If there are ten to twenty saints in a home meeting, we may sometimes bring them to attend the Lord's table meeting at the meeting hall on the Lord's Day morning. I believe this will be a great encouragement to them. Both the newly saved ones and those who have been saved for a long time will blend together in the meeting and be mutually encouraged. Still, we need to bear in mind that this is not a set regulation but is something entirely organic and flexible. This requires us to observe the situation and contact, fellowship with, and pray with the brothers in the districts or the meeting halls.

Both the former way of meeting and the present new way require our exercise of flexibility. There is no dead regulation for us to follow. Rather, we must determine something according to the actual situation. If some brothers and sisters are newly baptized and are meeting in a few homes, they should remain in their home meetings for a month or two. By the time the number in their district increases to thirty, forty, fifty, or sixty, we can lead them to set up a corporate district meeting. They do not necessarily have to go to the meeting hall. We may choose a house among them with a larger living room for the saints nearby to meet together corporately. These matters do not have to be arranged by the elders. As long as the saints in the district fellowship and pray according to the real situation and need, the thirty to sixty people can meet together. After three to four weeks we can bring these brothers and sisters to the meeting hall to attend the Lord's table meeting on the Lord's Day.

THE PROSPECT OF THE PROGRESS OF THE NEW WAY

The result of this practice will be encouraging. In the future there will be people here in Taipei attending different kinds of meetings on the same Lord's Day. Some will meet in homes, some in the districts, some in the meeting halls, and still others in the stadium. This is my long-term view. If the Lord has mercy on us, I hope He will grant us a big meeting hall that can accommodate ten thousand people for the blending of the saints.

Our view has to be broadened. If we want to increase our number and propagate the Lord's recovery, we must take this new way. As we all realize, if we take the old way, we will be bound in fetters and confined, and there will be no way out. May the Lord bless us.

(A message given on March 31, 1987 in Taipei, Taiwan)

CHAPTER FOURTEEN

HOME MEETINGS
AND THE USE OF *LIFE LESSONS*

(4)

BEING SPECIFIC IN USING *LIFE LESSONS*

Home meetings are the emphasis of the new way in the
Lord's recovery, and the most important thing for the home
meetings is knowing how to use *Life Lessons*. Our problem is
that when we use *Life Lessons,* we add too many of our own
words. This is like towing an old car behind us when we drive;
it distracts our concentration and causes trouble. For this
reason, it is often a help not to bring our Bibles, hymnals, and
tracts with us when we go to the home meetings. To bring all
these is to bring the "old car" with us. A successful salesperson is trained not to show two products to the buyer at the
same time. Once the customer finds out that there are more
products, he will want to see them all, even if there are hundreds of them. This makes it very hard for the salesperson.

Why do we say that it is often a help not to bring our
Bibles to the home meetings? It is because when we bring the
Bible with us, we are tempted to use some verses which are
not necessary for the lesson, and eventually we are distracted
from the main theme. The chapter we read may be about calling upon the name of the Lord, but we will be tempted to read
Genesis 1 about God's creation. After listening to us for a long
time, the ones in the home will be confused.

THE IMPORTANT "WEAPONS" FOR CONTACTING PEOPLE

Before the introduction of the Lord's new way, we needed
to collect various materials for gospel preaching. For this

purpose, the Gospel Bookroom published many gospel tracts, booklets, stories, and testimonies. However, not many people were baptized through our speaking of those stories and the testimonies quoted from classical writings. Based upon our experience, we studied this new way and discovered that what we had in the past was only like an oxcart, or at best a bicycle or rickshaw. It could not meet the present need of man's heart. Eventually, we compiled a gospel booklet entitled *The Mystery of Human Life,* which covers God's creation, man's fall, Christ's redemption, and God's dispensing. Those who have used this gospel booklet can testify that there is no need to talk about other items. All we need to do is open *The Mystery of Human Life* and read it with people. Then they will believe and be baptized very quickly.

Warfare throughout the world today can be regarded as a competition of weapons. The focus of every nation is to develop its own weapons and then negotiate over them, hoping that their own nation will possess the best weapons in the world. Because of this, national defense takes the biggest and highest share of most nations' budget. There is a Chinese proverb that says, "Good tools are the prerequisite for the success of a task." This is in the same principle as modern weapons. Therefore, today when we go to knock on doors, we should not bring extra items that are not our direct weapons. Our weapon for preaching the gospel is *The Mystery of Human Life,* and the one for leading the home meetings is *Life Lessons.* We need to be familiar and well-versed in these two weapons.

SEVERAL KEY POINTS
CONCERNING THE USE OF *LIFE LESSONS*

We may have apprehended this principle in a superficial way, but I am afraid that when it comes to practice, our mind still contains many extra things. *Life Lessons* is rich in content and abounds in verses. These very verses can be our temptations when using the lessons. We can compare using the verses to scratching an itch. Sometimes before we scratch, we do not feel much itching, but once we start to scratch, we itch more. Eventually our whole body begins to itch without remedy. When we use *Life Lessons,* we should not "scratch the itch." There is no need to talk about Genesis, Revelation, all four Gospels, and finally the Song of Songs. This is to scratch all the itching places; there is not enough time for that. In order to manage our time, we need to avoid this. The key for reading is simply to follow the content of the lessons. There is no need to add any explanation. In particular, we should never extend the meaning of the text or develop an understanding based on inference. We simply should read the content of the lesson with the new ones. If we come to a point we do not understand, we simply need to repeat-read, emphasize-read, vitalize-read, and pray-read. This will take care of many "itches."

In using the lesson books, we should first make good use of the verses. For example, Genesis 1:1 says, "In the beginning God created the heavens and the earth." We need to impart these words into people: "in the beginning," "God," "created," "the heavens," and "the earth." Not even one hundred long messages will be able to leave as much impression on the new ones. If we first impart the verses into people, they will receive the supply, because the Word of the Lord is living and powerful.

Second, we have to impart the footnotes and explanations of the quoted verses into people. Although we cannot say that every word in the footnotes is a gold nugget, each word is at least concise, to-the-point, and pertinent. Therefore, no further explanation is required. On the contrary, once we try to explain, we will dilute the meaning. This will be like adding too much water to a bowl of beef soup until it loses all its taste. We may think that our explaining helps people to understand. Little do we realize that our explanation actually dilutes the precise meaning.

In addition, we should never add extra content to the lessons. If we read a certain chapter, we should simply read that chapter and not make references to other books or materials. We should avoid doing this. Do not be afraid to repeat-read, emphasize-read, vitalize-read, and pray-read. Rather, we should pay attention to and strengthen these things. We must be sure to study *Life Lessons* in our private time and become familiar with its content. In so doing, when we are in the home meetings, we can spontaneously utter words from our mouths as from the pen of a ready writer, and whatever we speak will be the word in the lessons. We need to practice until this is the case.

BEING FAITHFUL AND STEADFAST IN DOOR-KNOCKING AND ATTENDING THE HOME MEETINGS

Whether or not we serve full-time in the future, as long as we serve the Lord, we need to do two things. The first is to go door-knocking by using *The Mystery of Human Life,* and the second is to have home meetings by using *Life Lessons.* In a restaurant that sells dumplings, some people do nothing else the whole day except make dumplings. Even if they find this boring, they still have to do it because this is their job. Some among us have become "addicted" to going out to knock on doors and baptize people. However, this is just the "honeymoon." Once the honeymoon is over, they may find it boring, just like the dumpling makers who, after making several thousand dumplings, have no more desire for it. In the future, though, the full-timers should simply go out to "make more dumplings," that is, to knock on doors to read *The Mystery of Human Life* with people and to carry out the home meetings by using *Life Lessons.*

An elderly brother among us said that according to his observation, the co-workers in the past had almost nothing to do except give messages from the podium, fellowship, visit churches, and visit people with problems. Apart from these things, he could not see what else they had done. However, it is different now. Every full-timer must not be idle and has no way to be idle. For this reason, this elderly brother was willing to serve full-time. If we want to serve the Lord full-time, we also should be like this. Seven days a week from the morning until night we should either knock on doors and baptize people or have home meetings to nourish and supply them. The more babies a mother has, the busier she will be. At the present time twenty thousand people have been baptized in our midst. They all need us to go to their home to nourish and take care of them.

Farmers do almost the same work all year long, which

seems very tedious. They sow in spring, plow in summer, harvest in autumn, and rest in winter. It is the same year after year. Every proper business is also like this. Every proper business in the world is tedious. Accountants find their job tedious because they deal with figures all day long. Computer technicians may have some pleasure in their work at first, but after doing it for a long period of time, they also will find nothing special in it. Computers are not smarter than the human mind created by God, so this line of work will also become tedious. Being a teacher is tedious, and being a doctor is also tedious. Every line of business is tedious.

Whatever we do is always interesting in the beginning, but after doing it for a long time, we find it boring. Husbands, wives, fathers, and children all become tired of what they do. However, all these tedious businesses are the proper business and proper occupations of human life. Therefore, we must be steadfast in door-knocking and having home meetings. This is the way ordained by the Lord, and this is our proper occupation.

THE RESULT AND ESTIMATES OF THE CHANGE OF SYSTEM

In the past, one church may not have brought even fifteen people to be saved and baptized each year, and even if fifteen people were baptized, perhaps not even five would remain. For this reason, we changed the system. Because of the change of the system, in one recent month we baptized one hundred sixty people. Although we are still inadequate in many areas, this result is sufficient enough to encourage us.

We have estimated that if we gain two thousand people through door-knocking, about one-fourth will remain, which is five hundred people. Every kind of production has a certain amount of loss and damage. In an orchard, for example, not all the fruit is harvested; at least one-third is sacrificed. While the trees are blossoming and bearing fruit, it may hail, or the birds may come and eat a certain amount. Only the fruit that is not damaged will be distributed to the markets for sale. It is the same with the production of cars. Not every car out of one hundred that are produced will be qualified. It may be fortunate if only eighty cars are qualified. Every kind of production has its sacrifices.

Recently when we were making our estimates, we were greatly encouraged. We never thought that the word spoken by the Lord in Matthew 13 and the principle of our estimation under His leading would be the same. In both cases, only one-fourth remain. In Matthew 13 the Lord spoke the parable of the sower. The first fourth of the seed fell beside the way and was immediately taken by Satan. This seed was altogether ineffective (v. 4). The second fourth fell on the rocky places where they did not have much earth. This kind of seed did not have deep roots and withered very quickly (vv. 5-6). The third kind grew a little deeper, but the thorns also came up. Then the anxiety of the age and the deceitfulness of riches utterly choked the word, causing it to become unfruitful (vv. 7, 22). Only the fourth kind, the last quarter, fell on the good earth and yielded fruit (v. 8). This portion of the Word shows us that even when the Lord Jesus worked on the earth, He gained only one-fourth of the people, and three quarters were lost.

We should be encouraged, rejoicing that the Lord has given us this way. According to this estimate, if we gain two thousand people through door-knocking, we will have five hundred people remaining who attend meetings regularly. Among these five hundred new ones who attend the meetings, we can produce one hundred twenty-five who will knock on doors. In this way, by the year 2000 the whole world can be covered and baptized. This is truly marvelous. Therefore, we should not lose heart but should be encouraged in the Lord.

HAVING A LONG-TERM VIEW IN TAKING THE NEW WAY

We know that the Lord Jesus is faithful to us. He spoke in the Gospel of Luke that He sends us out in the midst of the wolves, but among the wolves there are sons of peace who are pre-chosen by God (10:3-6). However, we need to be well prepared that some sons of peace may not remain to be sons of peace for their whole life. The name *Barnabas* in the New Testament means "son of encouragement." In the beginning, Barnabas was truly an encouragement to Paul. It was he who brought Paul into the New Testament ministry, and it was also he who brought Paul with him to go out to work. Eventually, though, he did not last long as an encouragement. Acts 15 shows us that Barnabas, this son of encouragement, because of his natural relationship in personnel matters, no longer worked together with Paul. This put Paul in a very difficult situation. Finally he separated from Paul (vv. 36-39), but the Lord sent Timothy to Paul, which caused him to be joyful.

We need to remember that no one can frustrate the Lord's way, but we also should not expect that this way will proceed smoothly without difficulty. Some have testified that after praying, confessing their sins, being filled, and going out, they baptized three to five families, and everything went smoothly. Others, however, fellowshipped that despite their effort no doors were open to them, or even when doors were opened to them, no one received the gospel. This truly caused them to despair. However, do not lose heart. We must believe that as long as we go out, there will be some profit. Do not worry about how many of the newly baptized ones will remain. It is a universally true principle that those who are optimistic are happy for everything, while those who are pessimistic worry about everything. We all should have an optimistic attitude and firmly believe that this way is the best way. No other way can gain so many people. Recently twenty thousand people have been baptized; even though eventually fifteen thousand are unstable, we still have gained five thousand people. Even among these five thousand there may be over three thousand who are weak, but there are still over one thousand who are stable. The joy in the universe is because of these one thousand.

Not all of our children are intelligent. If every child were intelligent, the world would be in disarray. If every American was capable of being the president, the world would be turned upside down. Americans would constantly contend one against another, and there would be no peace. We thank and praise the Lord that while some are intelligent, some are foolish. While we are taking this way, we should not look only at the dark side; we should also look at the bright side. In the Bible there is first evening and then morning (Gen. 1:5). This makes up one day. Everything has a bad side, but we should never be discouraged. Although we dare not say that this way is a broad highway without any difficulty, we know that this way is absolutely right and can be successful.

We may go out to knock on doors for the whole night, and no one may be baptized. We may go out again for a second night, and still no one may be baptized, and on the third night only two are baptized. It seems that we labored for the whole week for only two to be baptized. It was as if the Lord did not listen to our prayers. In actuality, though, this is more profitable than not going out at all. Moreover, the profit will be great because it will "snowball." Then in the future these compounded benefits will be added to our account. Therefore, do not be narrow-sighted or shortsighted. Rather, your vision should be broader and farther. This way is right. If we firmly believe this way and are faithful in taking it, after not too long the whole earth will be filled with our brothers and sisters.

If we consider the new way with this view, we will not be afraid if no one is baptized through our door-knocking, because today is not the only day in the universe. There are three hundred sixty-five days in a year, and we can always labor. Satan can never overcome us. He can cause us not to be able to gain people today and tomorrow, sending away all the sons of peace and giving us only wolves. In the end, however, we still will meet the sons of peace. Eventually, the Lord will add to us the lambs.

We are truly full of joy and hope within. There is no problem for us to go on. The Lord said, "Go in peace!" The work we are doing is a work of peace, the people we are seeking are the sons of peace, and the way we are taking is a way of peace. As long as we take this way, our success is assured.

(A message given on April 2, 1987 in Taipei, Taiwan)

CHAPTER FIFTEEN

HOME MEETINGS
AND THE USE OF *LIFE LESSONS*

(5)

The home meetings are the life-pulse of the church life and the key to the success of the new way. Therefore, we have to apply our full strength to the home meetings.

THE KEY TO THE SUCCESS OF THE HOME MEETINGS

Going with a Living Spirit

When we go to a home meeting, we must be living persons with a living spirit. If our spirit is not living, we had better not go. If we go, we will certainly give others an impression of emptiness and deadness, and this is what we must not do. When we go to the home meetings, we must be vital and go with our spirit. If we do not go with our spirit, we should not eat or sleep until our spirit is ready. Otherwise, we should not go at all. If you want to go to the home meetings, you must have the spirit and life.

Since the change of the system in October 1984, it has been our hope to have the small group meetings. However, in our opinion, the small group meetings are not successful, not in only one locality but in every locality, whether in Taiwan, Anaheim, Irving, or London. They have not been successful anywhere. There are two reasons for the meetings not to be successful. First, those who go to the small group meetings are deadened in their spirit. If a person goes to attend a big meeting or a "Sunday service," it does not really matter whether his spirit is dead or living and whether or not he goes with the spirit, because the leading ones are responsible for the meeting.

This is the reason why we are very hesitant about bringing the newly baptized ones to the big meetings. In the big meetings, some people may be falling asleep, while others may be talking or doing something else. We truly do not want the new ones to see that situation and be contaminated. If all of us still meet according to this old way, we too may eventually give up the meetings because we do not have the spirit and life. This is why we always emphasize that the home meetings must be living. If the home meetings are living, all the other meetings will also be living.

Some people may compare a meeting to a playground in which children jump and laugh; no one there is deadened. For the time being, we may agree to this saying, but even in a playground you still have to have a ball to play with. Likewise, in order to be living in the meetings we have to go with the spirit. It is ridiculous for players to come to the ball court without a ball. Without the ball, it is not possible to have the game. After our study, we have found that in the matter of bringing people to salvation, the ball is *The Mystery of Human Life,* and in leading the home meetings, the ball is *Life Lessons.*

Now although we have the ball, we still have another problem. The problem is that we do not know how to play; our playing is not up to the standard. This is what we are concerned about. What the coach fears most is that the ball, the court, the opponents, and everything else are ready, but the players cannot play well. This is a real headache for the coach.

We know that one ball game is different from another. On the court things are always changing, so each player has to receive training. When we use *Life Lessons,* we are the "players" who have to go through training. After the training, however, the way to play the game is not always the same. It is no wonder that no one among us truly knows how to play. Neither the elders, the co-workers, nor anyone else plays well because we have not received enough training.

Learning to Use the Spiritual Materials

The second reason that the small group meetings are not

successful is that we do not know how to use the spiritual materials. Since the beginning of the small group meetings in 1984, all the localities have realized that even though the meetings were good, there were no materials for the meeting. For this reason we compiled *Life Lessons*. Although we have had a very good response from everywhere concerning the materials, when many people use the materials, they either "miss the ball" or "throw it" where others cannot catch it. We still have the problem of not knowing how to use the materials. We can compare this problem to going to the market to buy groceries. People think that if they want to eat chicken, fish, vegetables, or rice, all they have to do is bring them home. They may have never realized that they do not know how to cook the rice. They may not even know where the kitchen knife is. When they see others preparing the water, stir-frying the vegetables, and doing other things, they may think it is simple, but when they try to do it themselves, they have all kinds of problems.

We cannot blame anyone but ourselves for not making good dishes. We think that as long as we have the groceries, we can all cook, open a restaurant, and be the chef. In actuality, everything is not as easy as we imagine. Similarly, we cannot say that because we have *Life Lessons,* we have a cure-all. Even if it is a cure-all, we have to know the right way to apply it. When we eat, we have to know how to take the food; we cannot put it into our ears or nostrils. Although we all are happy to have *Life Lessons,* we still have to consider how to use this publication.

THE FULL-TIMERS LEARNING TO GO DOOR-KNOCKING AND TO LEAD THE HOME MEETINGS

We already know where the secret lies. Today we have the ball, the coach, the court, and the players, but how are we going to play? We need to keep practicing. Therefore, all of us full-timers have to be clear that we are engaged in this profession to do two things: to go door-knocking and to lead home meetings.

In door-knocking, we must seek out the sons of peace. This may not be too difficult for us, but neither is it easy. When we first started door-knocking, it was popular among the localities, and everywhere it was so fresh. In Taipei especially, the saints knocked on almost all the doors neighboring the meeting halls. They knocked on the doors of some homes four or five times. This kind of plentiful door-knocking has both an advantage and a disadvantage. The disadvantage is that people may not like it when we keep knocking on their door. The advantage is that although they do not like it, they will admire our spirit and feel grateful for our love toward them. Perhaps when we first knock on someone's door, he does not open. When we go the second time, he may open the door, but his heart is not open. When we go a third and fourth time, he may open the door and also his heart, but he still will not be baptized. When we go the fifth time, however, he will be greatly touched and think that these people are truly amazing. They were rejected many times, but nothing could stop them from coming, not even the wind or the rain. With this one final contact, his heart is moved. A man's heart is not made of iron. If we knock on his heart a few more times, he may be softened and moved. Do not think that being rejected will spoil the matter. There is an advantage to it.

After knocking on every door, the situation will hardly be the same as it was before. The response may not be as good. Some may think that there are no more doors for them to knock on. However, in Taipei, for example, there are still many commuters whom we have not visited. Among them there are many sons of peace predestinated by God. Some of them are "sheep"; it is just that they have been influenced by the atmosphere of society and have put on a wolf's skin. Frankly speaking, God created them and prepared them as sheep. If we knock on doors a few more times, we will be able to pull off the wolf's skin and find the sheep.

We have not yet penetrated Taiwan with the gospel. It is not until we baptize all the people in Taiwan that we will have penetrated the whole land. We cannot deceive ourselves. The full-time serving brothers and sisters in particular need to be clear about this. To gospelize Taiwan, they should knock on doors not only in the big cities but also in the villages. Sometimes on the same day they may have to knock on the same door three times. In the morning they may knock on the door, but no one answers. Then at noon and again in the evening they may knock again without an answer. Therefore, they may need to go a fourth time. Perhaps no one is home until ten o'clock, so they can go again at that time. We need to be steadfast in door-knocking. Especially in the villages, if we practice door-knocking in the way that we are doing now, we may be able to knock on all the doors in one day. We need to knock on the same doors again and again. Only in this way can we gospelize Taiwan.

LEARNING TO USE *LIFE LESSONS* SKILLFULLY

The most important thing to learn for the home meetings is how to use *Life Lessons*. One of the characteristics of the four volumes of *Life Lessons* is that all the titles of the lessons are printed on the cover so readers will understand what the book is about at a single glance. For example, the first volume covers from lesson one, "Knowing That You Are Saved," to lesson twelve, "Knowing the Church." From this table of contents we can quickly see that the first volume is for helping the newly baptized ones to know that they are saved all the way to their knowing the church. The first lesson of the second volume is "Knowing the Sects," and the last lesson is "The Offering of Material Riches." The first volume covers from salvation to the church, while the second covers from sects to mammon. The first volume talks about knowing that you are saved, having the life of the Lord, knowing the church, and living a life in the church. All these are positive. However, on the negative side there are several "demons" that need to be dealt with. The first one is sects, and the last one is mammon. Thus, the second volume covers the teaching from sects to mammon. All of these matters are negative.

In the third volume, we have the positive side again. The first lesson is "Transferred into Christ," on being transferred from all the negative things into Christ. Being transferred into Christ is not being buried; it is a matter of living in Christ. The last lesson is "Raptured to Meet the Lord." Being transferred into Christ is being saved, while being raptured to meet the Lord is the end of our journey of following the Lord.

These twelve lessons cover the things from our being saved to the end of our journey. This is the content of the third volume.

The fourth volume begins with "The Way to Enjoy God's Salvation," that is, how to enjoy God's full salvation. Then lesson by lesson it speaks of the full salvation of God: the first stage of sanctification, the forgiveness of sins, the cleansing away of sins, propitiation, reconciliation, the second stage of sanctification, and justification. These are the aspects of redemption. Then there are also the aspects of life: regeneration, renewing, the third stage of sanctification, transformation, maturity, conformation, and the last item is glorification. In other words, all four volumes of *Life Lessons* range from knowing that we are saved to the obtaining of glory. Therefore, once the matters in all the forty-eight chapters are wrought into us, we will enter into glory. These forty-eight chapters clearly tell Christians all the matters from their being saved to entering into glory.

In addition to the above, we also need to practice our way of speaking. For example, when we go to a home meeting, we may want to tell the new ones, "Do you know what the first volume of *Life Lessons* covers? Let me tell you. It starts from knowing that you are saved and goes to knowing the church." Although this is not wrong, this way of speaking is like that of a student reciting for an examination. When we go to the home meetings, we should not speak in the way of giving high school lessons. We should bring people deeper and try our best to avoid the kind of questions and answers that students give. We should bear this in mind and abandon an "academic" atmosphere. University professors have their own way of teaching, which is different from the way the elementary teachers teach. We should not be elementary. We need to speak as if we were not quoting from *Life Lessons*. We should simply tell people that after knowing that they are saved, they should be in the church.

This kind of exercise may be too difficult for some people, but if it were not difficult, there would be no need for the full-timers to exercise and to learn. All the full-timers are college graduates. They have been in school for well over a decade. Today they are still receiving training here, but the content of this training is not chemistry, science, astronomy, geography, or history. It is door-knocking and home meetings. Many things we know without having learned them, but other things we may have been taught for over a year without knowing them. Therefore, we need a first term, a second term, a third term, and a fourth term in our training.

Basketball players know that even though there is only one ball, there are many different ways of playing. When I was young, I often watched basketball games, particularly those between the Chinese and the foreigners, because they played in many different ways. Some passed the ball by bouncing it on the floor, while some threw the ball high into the air. No matter how tall their opponents were, they had their own various techniques for winning the game. We must learn how to use *Life Lessons* until we can use the lessons skillfully. In this way, every time we have a home meeting, we will be able to reap a harvest.

We should obtain at least one copy of *Life Lessons* and study the lessons thoroughly. We should be able to memorize and speak from each of the forty-eight lessons. Then we will be so familiar with the content that when we go to the home meeting, we will not necessarily need to start with the first lesson. It will be like playing basketball. A player may not always pass the ball in the same direction. By playing differently each time, he can catch everyone off guard and throw the ball into the net. To do this, however, the players need to exercise to become skillful. We may find these few points easy to understand but difficult to practice. A coach has to teach his players the basic movements until they are not only familiar with them but can also exercise to become truly skillful players. If we are like this, then we will be successful when we go to the home meeting.

THE PREPARATION AND COMPILATION OF
FURTHER MESSAGES ON LIFE

In addition to compiling *Life Lessons,* we are also preparing to compile further messages on life, comprising two hundred forty topics, not in the format of lessons but of messages. There will be twenty volumes, each with twelve short messages. We cannot yet say that we know the topics for all the messages, but we already have the first ones. If the Lord wills, we will publish the first and possibly the second volume in the coming year. Since we all are busy putting out literature, none of us can live a life of leisure. To be sure, if we live a life of leisure, we will not be able to accomplish anything.

We should not think that full-timers lead a very comfortable life. History tells us that the ones who truly serve the Lord with their full time do not live comfortably. I hope that no one among us will quit after hearing this. The journey ahead is long, but we believe that we will have a prosperous future. Many of us have gone on in this way and passed through this kind of day. We all can testify that although we are busy and tired, we are full of joy and peace inwardly.

SOME FELLOWSHIP CONCERNING
THE PROGRESS OF THE HOME MEETINGS

When we go to a home meeting, we must learn to detect the atmosphere. In other words, we have to find out the real situation of the new ones and how much they have grown in life. Only in this way can we gradually lead them.

Although there are many points concerning leading the new ones, it is not necessary to practice them all immediately. We should first observe their situation. Then we can lead them accordingly. If the situation manifests the need for a certain kind of leading, and such a leading is possible, we can carry it out. However, if there is no such need or such a leading is not possible, we should wait for some period of time. We do not need to do things in a hurry. We may first lead a home to meet with two or three other homes. If one meeting a week is not sufficient for them, we can increase the frequency of the meetings. Perhaps we can add a Lord's table meeting, a prayer meeting, or a truth study meeting. This is one side of the matter.

On the other hand, we may feel that the new ones in this home meeting can be brought to a big meeting of the church. However, when we do this, we should not bring people from only three to five of the other home meetings. It is better to join with a number of other home meetings. We hope that when we bring them to the meeting in the meeting hall, we will bring at least twenty homes with about sixty brothers and sisters.

Before bringing them to the meeting, we first should train them by telling them, "Today we are going to see the big meeting in the church. This is the old meeting that we used to have, a meeting of our 'seniors.' It is hard for them not to have wrinkles or a certain taste of oldness. On the one hand, we are their younger generation and we should give them support and refresh them. Therefore, when we go, we should not shrink back or be overly reserved. We should refresh the atmosphere. When we break the bread with them, we should wash away the oldness with some 'fresh air.' On the other hand, no matter how old they are, they will eventually show their capability in the meeting. When they do this, we, the juniors, should receive from them and encourage each other to go on." We should learn to do this.

At the same time, all the ones who are leading the home meetings should learn to record in a chart the time and place of the meetings that they lead and the number in the meetings. The responsible brothers can then make a chart of statistics. There may be two thousand homes on the chart. The brothers should consider these two thousand homes carefully and find out to which meeting halls and districts these homes belong. It is best to make separate charts to list the names and numbers in each home meeting for every meeting hall and district and to keep a record of the new home meetings. The responsible brothers of every meeting hall need to keep the chart properly.

It will be good to make such a chart every month. We hope that every month there will be a record of increase and progress for an accumulative calculation. In this way, we can continue to show every meeting hall the result of our home meetings. In the future these results will be given to the brothers and sisters in every meeting hall who will lead the homes. Every church should also have a training to lead the brothers and sisters and perfect them appropriately so that they can go on with this service.

BEING LIMITED IN OUR AFFECTION
WHEN CONTACTING PEOPLE

Man is rich in feelings. If we do not see another person often, it is easy not to be irritated with him. People become irritated with each other when they see each other too often. The best way to avoid being upset with someone is to stop seeing him. After getting married, a husband and wife sometimes become upset with each other because they see each other so much, and some marriages eventually end in divorce. We can see this same principle in our contact with people. When we contact one another, we develop certain kinds of feelings.

When we first knock on the door of a home, the person there may open the door to us, but he may wear a cold face. Gradually, however, after knocking on his door a few more times, we eventually will baptize him. In this way, the relationship between us will change. He now will change from wearing a cold face to being grateful. He will feel that not only did we show grace to him and have love for him, but we also gave him the Lord, the truth of the Bible, light, life, and peace. In addition, we continued to visit him every week, especially after his baptism. It is natural that he would develop a certain feeling toward us. Some people develop particularly strong feelings. Some have wanted to give us everything. They prepared dumplings for us, gave us various items, and even suggested going on a picnic together. Therefore, we need to issue a warning about this. It is good to have feelings, but we should not have natural affection. Feelings are acceptable, but natural affection should be avoided. Feelings are a matter of mutual love. We may feel that a certain one is not only a man but now also a brother in the Lord. Not only so, it is we who begot this brother in the Lord. To be sure, we will have feelings toward him. However, this is where it should stop. We should not have natural affection. If we have natural affection, there will be trouble.

In the Old Testament proper feelings can be compared to frankincense in the meal offering (Lev. 2:1). This is what God wants. Frankincense is a kind of fragrance, but natural affection is honey in the meal offering, which God does not want (v. 11). God is pleased with frankincense but not with honey.

This is because frankincense will not rot, but honey ferments. This is the type in the Old Testament. In the New Testament the love in Christ can be compared to frankincense, while the natural affection of man is honey, which will ferment and cause trouble. Therefore, when we knock on doors to contact people, we should keep a limit.

However, we need to be balanced. Some have said that no matter how much they knocked on doors, the doors would not open, or even if the doors were open, the hearts were not. For others, however, good news came one door after another. They report that the many doors they knocked on were all open, or that a new home has been brought into baptism and is having meetings. These are two extreme responses, like the weather in the tropics and at the poles. From the results of our study, we have found that the brothers and sisters "at the poles" went out to knock on doors with a cold face. Their faces were expressionless. When people open the door and see a face like an iceberg, how can they avoid being frightened? We should not knock on doors in such a way. When we go out, we have to be "hot." Even before people come out to answer the door, we should already be smiling and rejoicing. Then when people open the door, they will be heated up. In this way it is normal that we will succeed.

We have to first train our character. If it is hard for someone to be "heated up," he needs to move from the "poles" to the "equator" to be warmed up by the hot air. If someone knocks on doors in this way, there will be no doors unopened. This is the main point of what we are saying. When we go out to work, whether it is door-knocking or visiting homes, we need to heat people up but not make them too hot. Making people feel too close to us is not appropriate, because when this kind of feeling comes, natural affection also follows. Feelings are acceptable, but natural affection is not.

When we are too hot, we need to stay in the cold for a while to cool ourselves down. We can have a feeling of love for others—we can even go on a picnic together—but in whatever we do, there must be a limit. We cannot fall into natural affection. The reason we are saying this is that we must go on with our work. If we fall into natural affection, the accomplishments through our previous efforts will come to nothing. This is why we must pay very special attention to this point.

(A message given on April 9, 1987 in Taipei, Taiwan)

CHAPTER SIXTEEN

HOME MEETINGS
AND THE USE OF *LIFE LESSONS*

(6)

THE CENTRAL LINE OF THOUGHT
IN *LIFE LESSONS*, VOLUME ONE

Life Lessons volumes one and two contain a total of eighteen topics, ten in volume one and eight in volume two. These two volumes have their own lines of thought. The first speaks from "Knowing That You Are Saved" to "Knowing the Church," while the second speaks from "Knowing the Sects" to "The Offering of Material Riches." Volume one begins with "Knowing that You are Saved" and "The Need of Your Whole Family to Be Saved," and continues with "Clearance of the Old Living," "Prayer," "Reading the Bible," and five kinds of knowing: "Knowing the True God," "Knowing Christ," "Knowing the Holy Spirit," "Knowing the Cross of Christ," and "Knowing the Church." The first three "knowings" are concerning the Father, the Son, and the Spirit; the other two are regarding the cross and the church. The line of thought here is that by knowing the Triune God—the Father, the Son, and the Spirit—and adding the cross, we have the church. Without the Father, the Son, and the Spirit, there is no church. Moreover, we may have the Triune God, yet without the cross there is still no church. If we have the Father, the Son, the Spirit, and the cross, the church will come forth.

Do not recite these topics in order to memorize them. It is only by grasping the line of thought that we can remember them. *Life Lessons* helps a new believer first to know that he himself is saved and second to see the need for his whole family to be saved. Then it helps him to clear his old living and leads him to pray and read the Bible. Then it helps him to begin to know the true God, Christ, the Holy Spirit, and also the cross of Christ, and even to know the church. We need to be familiar with all these topics. Do not wait until you go to take care of a home meeting to start reading the lessons and decide which topic is suitable. To do this is to sell ourselves cheaply. If a professor is still flipping through his books when he stands in front of the blackboard, he should be dismissed. When we go to take care of the home meetings, all these riches should already have been constituted in us in order to meet the instant and realistic needs.

THE CENTRAL LINE OF THOUGHT
IN *LIFE LESSONS*, VOLUME TWO

Volume two begins with "Knowing the Sects," "Meetings," and "The Bread Breaking Meeting." Then it continues with "Consecrating Ourselves," "Being Filled Inwardly and Outwardly with the Holy Spirit," "Preaching the Gospel," and "Serving the Lord," and it concludes with "The Offering of Material Riches." What volume one talks about are all positive things, but because of the fall and the desolation of the church, some negative things were brought in, and sects and denominations were produced. Therefore, we must lead the new ones to know the sects. Then we should help them to know that among the church meetings, the most important is the bread-breaking meeting. After having home meetings for a period of time, we must lead them to break the bread, so it is a necessity for them to know about the bread-breaking meeting. At the same time, the new ones have probably touched the Lord's love in the meetings and are willing to consecrate themselves to the Lord. Therefore, we need to go on to speak about consecrating ourselves. After consecrating themselves to the Lord, they will wish to do something for the Lord, so they must exercise their spirit. The Spirit has two aspects; they must be filled with the Spirit both inwardly and outwardly. Then they have to preach the gospel for the Lord, serve the Lord, and offer their material riches.

Among the eight topics of volume two there are two items

concerning offering. One is consecrating ourselves, and the other is offering material riches. Consecrating ourselves comes first, and offering our material riches follows. We must let the Lord gain our being first and then our material riches. The scriptural basis for this is 2 Corinthians 8:5, where Paul said that the Macedonian believers "gave themselves first to the Lord, and to us through the will of God." The Macedonians had received much grace in the matter of material riches. The apostle Paul testified for them that before offering their material riches, they had already let the Lord gain them. They first subjected themselves to the Lord, and not only to the Lord, but also to the apostles who took the lead to serve the Lord. They first let the Lord and the apostles, who took the lead to serve the Lord, gain them.

Here we see that the Lord wants to first gain our being. He does not want to gain our material riches first. Robbers throughout the world are all covetous for other people's money. They do not want your being, but to be sure, they want your money. The Lord is much wiser. He comes not for our money; He comes to gain our being. Once a person is gained by the Lord, his money will also follow. As long as we first let the Lord gain us, we will spontaneously take the step of offering material riches. Therefore, we should first consecrate ourselves and then offer our material riches.

Consecrating ourselves and offering our material riches are out of the same source. The source and motivation for consecration is the Lord's love. One passage in the Old Testament says, "I love my master,...I will not go out free" (Exo. 21:5). We can be free. No one is binding us and forcing us to serve the Lord. However, because we love Him, we do not want to be free. Therefore, love is the motive of our consecration.

What exactly is the motive for our offering of material riches? If we study the eight topics in volume two in great detail, we will be able to see that the motivation is the inward filling and the outward filling with the Holy Spirit. Once a person is filled with the Holy Spirit, three things will result: preaching the gospel, serving the Lord, and offering material riches. Consecrating ourselves comes out of the Lord's love to us, while offering material riches comes out of the filling of the Holy Spirit. When the Holy Spirit fills us, not only will sins and the world leave, but our money will also go out. If someone says that he is filled with the Holy Spirit, but his money still stays in his pocket, then he has only half a filling, a filling only on the surface. If he is filled completely, his material riches will surely go out. Therefore, consecrating ourselves comes out of the Lord's love to us, while offering material riches comes out of the filling of the Spirit in us. Once we are filled, our material riches are "flushed" away. One is filling, and the other is flushing. The filling of the Holy Spirit will flush out our material riches.

As we lead the home meetings, we should never recite these topics in a rigid way. We should be very familiar with these topics inwardly, and our line of thought should be very clear. Then when we speak to others, we will be able to speak spontaneously. For this reason, before we go to labor on the home meetings, we must prepare ourselves well by first preparing the topic and then, if we have time, by reading through the content thoroughly.

BEING DILIGENT IN ADVANCING OUR STUDY AND NOT BEING SLOTHFUL

We have to encourage all the brothers and sisters serving in the literary work to further their studies, especially in the study of vernacular Chinese. In Chinese vernacular literature, as recommended by scholars in general, there are four excellent classics. The first is *All Men Are Brothers;* the second, *A Dream of the Red Chamber;* the third, *The Travels of Lao Ts'an: A Social Novel;* and the fourth, the Chinese Union Version Bible. A contemporary Chinese scholar, Hu Shih, said that the Chinese Union Version is a great advancement in Chinese vernacular literature. Therefore, it would be profitable for us to read the Chinese Union Version thoroughly. The greatest advantage of the Chinese Union Version is its beauty in rhythm. Romans 12:1 is an example of this beauty. The literary style of Ephesians is also very good, although from the viewpoint of the original meaning it was translated relatively poorly.

BUDGETING OUR TIME EFFECTIVELY

The full-time serving brothers and sisters need to pay special attention to budgeting their time, because they often express that they do not have enough time. We have already fellowshipped that full-timers, especially the younger generation, should do only two things full time. One is to visit people by knocking on their doors to lead them to believe in the Lord and be baptized, and the other is to have home meetings to nourish and take care of the new ones. The home meetings can be compared to economics, an all-inclusive subject. The greatest subject of learning in the world is economics, which includes not only military science, political science, and finance, but in its broader, cultural sense, all things related to literature, astronomy, geography, history, and so forth. Similarly, our home meetings are all-inclusive and require us to spend much time to learn.

Many of the full-time serving ones among us are about thirty years old. Out of twenty-four hours each day they sleep for at most seven hours. Then they use an hour for each meal time, including some rest, for a total of three hours a day. Since meals and sleeping use at most ten hours, they still have fourteen hours left in the day. If they use two hours for exercise and eight hours for work, according to the customary working hours, they will still have four hours of spare time. This is why the entertainment business in America is so prosperous. It takes advantage of people's spare time to make great profits in nightclubs, concerts, stage performances of all kinds, television, movies, traveling, and endless other types of entertainment.

However, people who play and exercise like this do not live a long life. We all know that it is good to exercise, but if we exercise excessively, we will die early. Experience tells us that good athletes often do not live beyond sixty years old. The reason many die early, such as those in Olympic sports, is that they exercise too rigorously. It is good to exercise for a short time, but to use too much time is not appropriate. In order to live long, we need to exercise for our health but not for entertainment.

There is a Chinese saying: "Long illness makes the patient a good doctor." Although we have not studied hygiene or medicine, from our illnesses and from the doctors and nurses who cared for us, we have learned how to stay healthy. We have learned that even though we need to spend time exercising, we should do it absolutely not for entertainment but for health. If we spend these four hours for entertainment, we will gradually be defiled by immoral and improper things. In America, many sins come from these four hours of entertainment. This is truly a terrible thing.

Here we see the importance of budgeting our time. Every day we spend seven hours sleeping and three hours taking meals. This is an easy schedule. Then we spend two hours in exercise and various activities, which is more than enough; actually, it is sufficient to spend only one hour exercising each day. In addition to the normal eight hours for working, the four to five hours remaining should be time for studying. We can study many books if we leave four to five hours a day. We should not only read books but also study them. We can study any good book. I have studied many books ever since I was a child, and I am still studying now. I study not only Chinese and English dictionaries but also Greek. I am still studying continually.

MEMORIZING *LIFE LESSONS* BEING BENEFICIAL FOR OUR WHOLE LIFE

The best way of studying is still the old Chinese method, which is the method of reciting. Children may not understand the meaning of what they study, but they are still able to recite the text: "Confucius said, 'Isn't it a pleasure to study and practice what you have learned?'" To them it seems that it is not very important whether or not they understand the content. It is still beneficial to them as long as they can recite it well. The study methods of the modern age are all fast; people learn quickly and forget quickly. If we look back from our graduation until now, we may realize that we have forgotten almost all the books we studied in elementary, junior high, high school, and college. According to the old Chinese learning method, however, children recite books from the first day they go to school. They recite from *The Three-character Classics, The Book of Family Names,* and *The Analects of Confucius* every day. The teacher teaches the students to recite word by word, and eventually the students are not able to forget them for their entire life because everything that they recite remains in them. Moreover, as time goes by and they grow older, they become more able to apply this knowledge in practice.

Today when we study the Bible, we should not aim at speed-reading. Rather, we should recite the verses with a serious attitude. However, we do not need to recite too quickly. If we memorize quickly, we will tend to forget quickly, and what we gain will not last long. I hope that we can all recite the four volumes of *Life Lessons*. We all need to make such an effort. We should memorize not only the main topics but also the contents under them. This is not a difficult task for young people. We have calculated that there are about three hundred sixty pages in the four volumes. If we recite one page a day for three hundred sixty-five days, we will have recited all of them in a year. When we were in secondary school, we recited *The Collection of Ancient Chinese Classic Literature*. The passages in this book are much longer than those in *Life Lessons*. There are not many lines on each page of *Life Lessons*, so we can recite at least two pages a day.

The young people who go to labor on a home meeting should make a determination regarding their practice. Starting from today, they should spend four months to study *Life Lessons*. There should be an examination every half month, and they should be able to recite six lessons. This will take care of twelve lessons in one month and forty-eight lessons in four months. We must work so thoroughly on the text that we are able to speak it fluently and the content of the lessons becomes our inward constitution. This must become our main emphasis. If we study these four volumes well before we go to labor on the home meetings, our viewpoint will be completely different.

Even if we have recited the whole of *Life Lessons*, we must speak, not recite, when we go out to visit people. There is no contradiction here. Because we speak after memorizing, all the riches are within us. Therefore, when we speak, we can speak fluently and smoothly. Moreover, every time before going to lead a home meeting, we need to pray, allow the Holy Spirit to fill us inwardly and outwardly, and be dealt with thoroughly. If this is the case, we can surely saturate Taipei so that in every home there is a meeting which is new and living.

Again we can use playing basketball as an example. If the players rigidly follow only what their coach has taught them about passing and catching the ball, they will certainly lose the game. In a real game the players cannot simply have memorized what the coach taught them. Instead, they should be familiar with what the coach has taught through regular practice. They should have practiced to the extent that all the skills have been wrought into their muscles. Then during a game the players will not play by memory or recitation. Rather, their muscles will have developed a spontaneous movement. Similarly, parents should teach their children when they are young so that what has been taught can be wrought into their "blood." Then it will be impressed deeply within them and will be difficult to forget. Therefore, we must memorize these four volumes of *Life Lessons*. They are essential, especially the scriptural quotations. There are about three hundred verses quoted in the four volumes. Most of these three hundred verses are from the New Testament. They may be considered the essence of the New Testament. If we can recite all these three hundred verses, the essence of the New Testament will be in us. This will benefit us for our whole life.

THE PROSPECT OF THE NEW WAY AND THE KEY TO ITS SUCCESS

From now on, the way the church should take is to knock on doors, lead people to be baptized, and set up home meetings. The regular church life is the home meetings. If in Taipei there are one hundred twenty thousand brothers and sisters who meet regularly and are reliable, their coming together to meet week after week will have a great impact here. This many brothers and sisters will comprise at least thirty to forty thousand families. Although we have not worked to this extent, we can already see that there are familiar faces everywhere. Therefore, we must work out the estimated number by the Lord's grace until there are nine hundred sixty thousand brothers and sisters living the Christian life in Taipei. This outlook seems unlimited, but it will be achieved one day.

I hope that every one of our brothers and sisters will have a normal living, proper attire, and an appropriately furnished home. If we are all proper and we spread throughout the different classes of society, the impact will be immeasurable. I believe that what the Lord said in Matthew 5 will be fulfilled. There the Lord said that the disciples are the salt of the earth (v. 13). The earth has been corrupted, but salt comes to kill the germs of corruption. The disciples are also the light of the world effacing the world's darkness (v. 14). We believe that within ten years this condition will appear. I hope the young people can all focus on this target. This is more valuable than anything else.

The key to success depends very much on our use of *Life Lessons*. We cannot go through these four volumes in one year. We estimate that although there are only forty-eight lessons, it takes one and a half years to complete this course. What we expect is that after one and a half years, after we have gone through all the forty-eight lessons of the four volumes of *Life Lessons,* the new ones we lead will become what we are, and the number of saints will double. If we multiply in this way, the people we gain will not be indifferent or like the "church members" in Christianity. The ones we gain will be solid.

We all today have studied in school. We have studied science, English, and many subjects. However, our parents, who were born many years earlier, did not have the environment or opportunity to study. Therefore, it is difficult and too harsh for us to demand that they learn what we know. It is the same in the church today. We cannot make harsh demands on the elderly brothers and sisters. However, we hope that the young full-timers will learn well, specifically to gain people wherever they go.

CONTACTING PEOPLE WITH A LONG-TERM VIEW

To others our door-knocking and visiting are like drinking

sweet and sour soup. When people first receive it, it is hot and sour, but after they receive it, they find it very sweet. When people see us neatly dressed and knocking on their door, they feel embarrassed if they do not open to us. However, once they open, they cannot get rid of us, and eventually we even baptize them in water, which is difficult for them to understand. Nevertheless, when they listen to us, they find that what we speak is real. What we are bringing to their home is a "diamond," and they feel it would be a pity if they did not receive it. That is why our visiting is like sweet and sour soup. Furthermore, people may think that if they receive what we speak, that will be enough. But then we begin a home meeting, which brings them not only the Lord Jesus but also the Bible. That is why they may show us a long face when we first come, but after talking with us for five minutes, their face relaxes. Then after talking for another five minutes, they begin to smile, and after ten more minutes they will pray, sing hymns, and thank and praise the Lord together with us. Finally, they will even make an appointment with us for the next visit. This is all our experience.

After they see us off, however, they may reconsider what has just happened, and they may start to doubt. On the one hand, they believe, but on the other hand, they may doubt. After doubting they believe again, and after believing they have doubts again. As long as you are a Christian, you will have this kind of experience. It is like someone who grinds in a mill; first he pushes the grindstone in one direction, and then he pushes it in the other. When you have gained more experiences, the Lord Jesus will make even more trouble for you. In the past we were free to watch movies, play sports, and travel around freely wherever we desired. However, it is now different. The Lord in us often objects to this and disagrees with that, which makes us feel uneasy within.

We all have had these experiences after believing in Jesus. We are progressing or backsliding, going up or down all the time. Moreover, on this path there are many temptations, especially after we have started to serve the Lord full time. When we look at ourselves, we find ourselves meeting today, meeting tomorrow, and serving the day after, but no matter what we do, we will never get rich. Some of our classmates have become great in the exporting business or as contractors, but we are still poor preachers loving the Lord and thanking and praising Him every day. Others can hardly understand this. In 1944 I needed to recuperate from an illness for two and a half years, and I was alone in Tsingdao for the last one and a half years. Because of my tuberculosis, I could not walk for a very long distance. One day as I took my cane and went for a walk in the scenic area of Tsingdao, I was complaining and feeling sorry for myself. I considered that I was empty-handed, possessing nothing, and without my family. I felt that I had nothing at all. It was at that very moment that the Lord operated in me again and made me joyful. Then I began to thank and praise Him because I knew that what I had gained was the most precious thing in the universe. People in the world pursue after houses, land, and other things, which are dung. The only truly valuable thing is to gain the Lord.

Do not be afraid that the newly saved ones will have fluctuating feelings. Man's feelings are like the weather; if the weather is not good, after a couple of days it will be sunny again. Do not look only at people's outward condition. It does not matter if they are not joyful today because they will be joyful again tomorrow. Moreover, we who serve the Lord should have a long-term view, because there will be a time when people come to the end of their life. At that time everyone who believes in the Lord will see that what he has done has been very valuable. When someone approaches death, he will understand that houses, companies, and money do not count. All that is valuable is the Lord deep within him. There is nothing more valuable than what we do. We need to be encouraged by this good prospect that there will be Christians everywhere meeting in different homes.

FELLOWSHIP CONCERNING
THE PRACTICE OF THE HOME MEETINGS

At this stage when we go to labor on the home meetings, we must pay attention to the situation of the family and understand how many meetings they are able to have. Generally speaking, there should be a meeting once a week in a home, but this is not enough for the long run. However, we should not add more meetings immediately. If we add too many meetings, it will be too much for them. We need to adjust the meetings according to the actual situation, and we should consider which meeting should be added—the Lord's table meeting, prayer meeting, fellowship meeting, or truth meeting. This requires our observation.

Furthermore, we should not treat all the new ones in the same way. After they are saved, some people grow faster and have a greater capacity, so we should feed them more. We should never be like the schools that offer the same curriculum to all the classes. This does not work. Today the good schools throughout the world take note of the talented students and put them in separate classes. We must observe people's inward condition of pursuing, fulfill their desire for pursuing, and add suitable meetings for them. This is the first point.

The second point is concerning the need of the new ones to know the church. Some newly baptized ones disappear one or two months after being baptized. We think that they have backslidden, but actually they have not. According to the normal thought and social custom, they suppose that after being baptized they should go to a "church" for a Sunday service. One brother testified recently that when he went to visit a family of new ones on the Lord's Day, they were about to go out to find a church for this purpose. This is an example of how some newly baptized ones may not have a strong will to pursue, but they still have the thought that as new Christians they should look for a church to settle down in. We must not overlook this situation. We should immediately bring this type of new ones to the meeting hall to join the meetings. Otherwise, once they go to the denominations and join their meetings, they will feel that they have what they were looking for.

It is too extreme to be concerned that the new ones will be contaminated by the old meetings. We need to be balanced. Once we realize that someone wants to participate in the church, we should grasp the opportunity, bring them to the meeting hall, and speak the truth to them concerning the church. In the New Testament Paul tells us that we admonish every man and teach every man in all wisdom that we may present every man full-grown in Christ (Col. 1:28). We do not have only one method to lead people. Rather, we should give people the way to move forward based on their condition.

For the general regular meetings, we should meet in the homes as home meetings. Then we should bring the new ones to the meeting hall once every two or three weeks. Before coming to the meeting hall, we need to prepare them and let them know that in the home meeting we all function and speak freely according to the Spirit, and we should do the same when we attend the meeting in the meeting hall. They should not regard the meeting hall as a place for them to be a guest and go merely to visit. This is wrong. When we go to the meeting hall, we also need to follow the Spirit's leading to release our spirit to praise and pray. We need to gradually let those we lead in the home meetings be connected with the church.

LEARNING ABOUT HOME MEETINGS IN ALL ASPECTS

We should not be too rigid when leading the home meetings. On the one hand, when we go to the home meetings, we do not need to say anything new. For the preaching of the gospel we use *The Mystery of Human Life,* and for establishing the home meetings we use *Life Lessons.* On the other hand, though, we need to be flexible. We can spend some time before the home meeting, or eight to ten minutes afterward, for answering questions. Some new ones may want us to stay a little longer, and some may want to ask us about various matters. Moreover, they may be persistent about finding the answers. Such times are the best opportunities for us to infuse something into them.

For example, someone may ask what the church really is and where it comes from. Then we should explain in detail. Everyone wants to be clear about his origin, where he comes from; this is normal. Likewise, today when people are saved, they have the thought that they have received a religion, so they will wish to know how this religion originated. If someone asks us this question, he is offering us the opportunity to help him. Whether or not we are able to answer makes a big difference. If we do not explain well, we will misrepresent ourselves, giving the new one a wrong concept. Although he listens to what we speak, he may not understand due to our unclear explanation, and he may not come anymore. Even if he was baptized by us and is actively pursuing the Lord, due to our unclear explanation he may think that he should not join such a group. Therefore, our daily equipping is very important.

I believe at least half of the families are willing to spend time to talk to us. If they are too busy today, there will still be a chance the next time. If they ask about certain practical matters, we should sit down and spend ten or twenty minutes to clearly explain the matters to them. Many times people may not have specific questions, but we should still learn to lead them to the spiritual points. For example, a new one may ask, "Is it sufficient just to believe in the Lord?" This kind of question is a very good opportunity to lead people to know their spirit within. We can explain that after believing in the Lord, we need to follow the Lord and serve Him. Moreover, our following the Lord and serving Him focuses not on the outward things but on following the spirit within us. From this point, we can go on to talk about the spirit. All these things require our observation.

We need to see that learning to lead the home meetings is like learning economics. Economics is ever-changing and all-inclusive. Industry and all things in a society can be affected by the weather, the harvest, and the food supply; the study of economics deals with all these matters. The outbreak of wars, the situation in the world, and the budget for national defense are also included in economics. This illustrates that to labor on the home meetings can be complicated and ever-changing. Therefore, the more we know and the more properly we use the home meetings, the more effective we will be.

We also need to realize that a person's word exposes him. When we visit a person, what we are most concerned about is if he will not speak. Once he speaks, even if he speaks only one word, we can know his inward condition so as to meet his inward needs. We should learn to discern the different types and natures of people. Some people are outgoing, some are quiet, some are strict, and some are easy-going. We have to know all these things. After knowing people, we should know what to speak to them. Even though we may be teaching the same curriculum, we may use one method to teach one type of person and another method for another person. What we speak to different types of people is different, because everyone's nature, stature, disposition, conduct, facial expressions, and manner of speaking are different. We cannot treat everyone in the same way.

THE PROSPECT OF THE NEW WAY BEING ENDLESS

The results of knocking on doors and laboring on the home meetings are endless. So far, it seems that the home meetings are not as fruitful as door-knocking, but this is a wrong concept. In the near future we will see that the effectiveness of the home meetings far exceeds that of door-knocking. When we labor on a home, we gain a home; this will continue like a link in a chain and be powerful. However, it all depends on how we labor. There is a saying, "A burning fire does not fear being fierce." When we go out to labor on home meetings, we are fanning the fire into flame, and we do not fear that it will be too fierce. We have to stir up all the new ones. We should know that when we labor on a home, a home will be enlivened and raised up. We only need to fan the flame until all the old and young ones rise up, and at that time we will succeed. May the Lord bless all that we do and the going on of the new way.

(A message given on April 14, 1987 in Taipei, Taiwan)

CHAPTER SEVENTEEN

HOME MEETINGS
AND THE USE OF *LIFE LESSONS*

(7)

THE CENTRAL LINE OF THOUGHT
OF *LIFE LESSONS*, VOLUME THREE

The general subject of *Life Lessons,* volume three is "Transferred into Christ." When we are transferred into Christ, we are then "Joined to Christ," "Abiding in Christ," "Experiencing Christ," expressing Christ, and "Taking Christ as Everything" (lessons twenty-five through twenty-nine). After that, we are "One Spirit with the Lord," "Living in the Fellowship of Life," "Obeying the Sense of Life," "Obeying the Teaching of the Anointing," and "Walking according to Spirit" (lessons thirty through thirty-four). In this way, we are "Awaiting the Lord's Coming" so that we can be "Raptured to Meet the Lord" (lessons thirty-five and thirty-six). When we are transferred into Christ to live a life that is sanctified, spiritual, overcoming, and one spirit with the Lord, we will eagerly await the Lord's coming and will be raptured to meet Him and be with Him joyfully. This is the line of thought in volume three.

THE CENTRAL LINE OF THOUGHT OF
LIFE LESSONS, VOLUME FOUR

Volume four is altogether on the complete salvation of God. The first lesson speaks of "The Way to Enjoy God's Salvation." Although this lesson does not specifically mention each aspect of salvation, it includes the first stage of sanctification. This first stage of sanctification is the first step of the way to enjoy God's salvation. Secondly, it is "The Forgiveness of Sins and the Cleansing Away of Sins" and "Propitiation and Reconciliation." Following this is "Sanctification—the Second Stage," "Justification," and "Regeneration." The forgiveness of sins, the cleansing away of sins, propitiation, reconciliation, sanctification, and justification are the six steps of preparation, the result of which is regeneration. When we have the first six steps, we can then be regenerated. After regeneration we have "Renewing" and "Sanctification—the Third Stage," followed by "Transformation," "Maturity," "Conformation," and eventually, "Glorification."

Hence, the four volumes of *Life Lessons* cover from "Knowing That You Are Saved" to "Glorification." In brief, they cover our being saved to our being glorified.

A DEMONSTRATION OF THE USE OF *LIFE LESSONS*

The content of *Life Lessons* is deeper from one volume to the next, but this does not mean that there is nothing profound in the first volume. For example, lesson nine in volume one is the continuation of the previous lesson concerning "Knowing Christ." This lesson speaks mainly of knowing Christ's person and also His work. The incarnation of Christ was a work, His crucifixion was a work, His resurrection from the dead was a work, and His ascension was also a work.

The second lesson on knowing Christ begins with His ascension to the heavens and continues with His heavenly ministry. This part of the work of Christ is very deep for many Christians. Today very few Christians know that Christ is accomplishing His heavenly ministry. Almost all Christians know that Christ bore our sins on the cross, died for us, gave Himself up for us, and shed His blood for us, yet very few know His heavenly ministry. There are not even many professors of theology, pastors, or preachers who properly know this.

Repeat-reading, Emphasize-reading, Vitalize-reading, and Pray-reading

Because this lesson is so profound and high, we must be particularly careful in using it when we go to the home meetings. We do not need to speak too much or spend too much effort on this lesson. According to the lesson, we can simply say, "But now He has obtained a more excellent ministry inasmuch as He is also the Mediator of a better covenant" (Heb. 8:6). Then we can continue to explain, "After Christ enacted the new covenant (Matt. 26:28) through His death on the earth, He ascended to the heavens to be the Mediator of this new covenant, executing it upon those who believe in Him" (p. 61). Hence, people can at least see that the Lord Jesus has a ministry in the heavens today, and this ministry is for Him to be the Mediator of the new covenant. He not only ensures that the new covenant will not fail, but He also executes this new covenant upon those who believe in Him.

The Lord Jesus has accomplished the new covenant, and now He is the Mediator of the new covenant in the heavens, executing the new covenant that He accomplished upon you and me, who believe in Him. If there are any who do not understand this, we should fellowship more with them, lead them to repeat the related words in the lesson, and read with them in a living way. Lastly, we need to lead them to pray with us. If they say that they do not know how to pray, we should lead them to follow our prayer sentence by sentence.

Never Extending the Meaning of the Text or Developing an Understanding Based on Inference

Although these matters are deep, some who are desirous to pursue the Lord may have the heart to understand, and they may raise an endless stream of questions. We should pay attention to this. On these occasions, we should never extend the meaning of the text or develop an understanding based on inference, turning to the life-study messages or other publications. We should simply use the materials in the lessons lest we be lost in the "forest."

If someone continues to raise questions and refuses to let us go, we should treasure such a heart and repeat the lesson once again. If he still does not let us go, we should speak to him one more time. We need to believe that the more we fellowship, the more he will understand. Then he will receive an impression of the new covenant and know that the Lord Jesus is the Mediator of the new covenant and that He is now in the heavens doing one thing, that is, executing the new covenant upon those who believe in Him. The more we do this, the more people will be impressed.

Depending on the Work of the Holy Spirit

When we touch the Lord's word, we must know that the Lord's word and the Lord's Spirit are inseparable. Therefore, we should not depend as much on our explanation as on the work of the Holy Spirit. As we continue to repeat-read, vitalize-read, and pray-read, the Holy Spirit will do a work along with the word to open the mind within men and cause them to understand the word. Perhaps as someone reads with us three or four times, his inner being will suddenly be opened and made clear to know that the Lord Jesus is the Mediator, executing the new covenant He accomplished for him. Regardless of the situation, we need to be patient with people. If they do not let us go, we should be happy for their pursuing heart, and we should read again to get into the words with them.

Sometimes, perhaps after we leave, someone may continue to be perplexed. However, we should believe that the Holy Spirit will work in him. This is very wonderful. Some may be enlightened in three to five days, but some may still not understand after three to five months. Still, there will be a day in which each person will be enlightened because something has been injected into him, that is, that the Lord Jesus is the Mediator of the new covenant and that today He is in the heavens, executing the new covenant upon us. Sooner or later, this will be very clear to the new ones, and it will have a great impact upon them.

We need to realize that most of the newly baptized ones have been saved within the past few months and that they do not know much. Therefore, we should try not to use too much of the material in volumes three and four. We should teach the first two volumes to lay a foundation in them before starting to use the topics in the next two volumes. We should avoid trying to teach them the content of volumes three and four at the beginning, because they have not yet reached that level.

CHOOSING A SUITABLE TOPIC FOR THE NEW ONES— AN ILLUSTRATION OF THE USE OF VOLUME FOUR

In spite of what has been said, there are a few lessons in volume four that can be used as references. For example, in lesson thirty-seven "The Way to Enjoy God's Salvation," there are three main points—the sanctification of the Holy Spirit, our repentance, and our believing and being baptized. This lesson mentions that after a person is separated from the world unto God and is moved in his heart, he will repent, believe, and be baptized. This material can easily be used in the home meetings.

This is also a suitable lesson to help those who are newly saved to know how the Spirit searches, enlightens, moves, and separates people while they are still sinners. This is the sanctification of the Holy Spirit. Because the Holy Spirit touches man in this way, we sinners can be awakened and repent. This is revealed to us in the Gospel of Luke. Luke 15 speaks of a woman who lost a silver coin. She lit a lamp, swept the house, and sought carefully until she found it (v. 8). It is by the Holy Spirit's enlightening and searching within man in such a way that a sinner is awakened to repent. John 16 also says that when the Holy Spirit comes, He will convict the world concerning sin and concerning righteousness and concerning judgment (vv. 8-11). All these verses speak of the work of the Holy Spirit in sinners to enlighten, move, search, and cause them to have the thought to turn to God.

Luke 15 continues with another parable, the parable of the prodigal son. This prodigal son who left the father's house was feeding hogs, and one day he came to himself and said, "How many of my father's hired servants abound in bread, but I am perishing here in famine!" (v. 17). That he came to himself is based upon the woman's lighting the lamp and searching in the previous parable. This woman is the Holy Spirit. The Holy Spirit comes to enlighten and search so that the sinner, who is far away from the father's house, can come to himself. This is the meaning of repentance. This illustrates that before we go to the home meetings, we must study the content of *Life Lessons*. Only then when we contact people can we know their inward needs and give them the proper help.

Lesson thirty-eight in volume four speaks about "The Forgiveness of Sins and the Cleansing Away of Sins." All the saved ones should know that God forgives their sins and cleanses their unrighteousness. Following this, lesson thirty-nine speaks about "Propitiation and Reconciliation." These are also things that the saved ones should know. Next is "Sanctification," which is a little deeper, and "Justification," which also is deeper. These matters should be taught gradually. However, lesson forty-two, on "Regeneration," is a lesson many newly-baptized ones should know clearly.

The above gives us the general idea that although these lessons are from volume four, some can still be used right away. The latter part of volume four, which covers "Renewing" after regeneration, "Sanctification—the Third Stage," "Transformation," "Maturity," "Conformation," and "Glorification," should not be touched at this point. Perhaps we should wait for eight months to a year to cover these. In any case, the decision must be made according to the actual condition of those in the home meeting.

(A message given on April 21, 1987 in Taipei, Taiwan)

ABOUT THE AUTHOR

Witness Lee was born in 1905 in northern China and raised in a Christian family. At age 19 he was fully captured for Christ and immediately consecrated himself to preach the gospel for the rest of his life. Early in his service, he met Watchman Nee, a renowned preacher, teacher, and writer. Witness Lee labored together with Watchman Nee under his direction. In 1934 Watchman Nee entrusted Witness Lee with the responsibility for his publication operation, called the Shanghai Gospel Bookroom.

Prior to the Communist takeover in 1949, Witness Lee was sent by Watchman Nee and his other co-workers to Taiwan to ensure that the things delivered to them by the Lord would not be lost. Watchman Nee instructed Witness Lee to continue the former's publishing operation abroad as the Taiwan Gospel Bookroom, which has been publicly recognized as the publisher of Watchman Nee's works outside China. Witness Lee's work in Taiwan manifested the Lord's abundant blessing. From a mere 350 believers, newly fled from the mainland, the churches in Taiwan grew to 20,000 in five years.

In 1962 Witness Lee felt led of the Lord to come to the United States, settling in California. During his 35 years of service in the U.S., he ministered in weekly meetings and weekend conferences, delivering several thousand spoken messages. Much of his speaking has since been published as over 400 titles. Many of these have been translated into over fourteen languages. He gave his last public conference in February 1997 at the age of 91.

He leaves behind a prolific presentation of the truth in the Bible. His major work, *Life-study of the Bible,* comprises over 25,000 pages of commentary on every book of the Bible from the perspective of the believers' enjoyment and experience of God's divine life in Christ through the Holy Spirit. Witness Lee was the chief editor of a new translation of the New Testament into Chinese called the Recovery Version and directed the translation of the same into English. The Recovery Version also appears in a number of other languages. He provided an extensive body of footnotes, outlines, and spiritual cross references. A radio broadcast of his messages can be heard on Christian radio stations in the United States. In 1965 Witness Lee founded Living Stream Ministry, a non-profit corporation, located in Anaheim, California, which officially presents his and Watchman Nee's ministry.

Witness Lee's ministry emphasizes the experience of Christ as life and the practical oneness of the believers as the Body of Christ. Stressing the importance of attending to both these matters, he led the churches under his care to grow in Christian life and function. He was unbending in his conviction that God's goal is not narrow sectarianism but the Body of Christ. In time, believers began to meet simply as the church in their localities in response to this conviction. In recent years a number of new churches have been raised up in Russia and in many eastern European countries.

OTHER BOOKS PUBLISHED BY

Living Stream Ministry

Titles by Witness Lee:

Abraham—Called by God	0-7363-0359-6
The Experience of Life	0-87083-417-7
The Knowledge of Life	0-87083-419-3
The Tree of Life	0-87083-300-6
The Economy of God	0-87083-415-0
The Divine Economy	0-87083-268-9
God's New Testament Economy	0-87083-199-2
The World Situation and God's Move	0-87083-092-9
Christ vs. Religion	0-87083-010-4
The All-inclusive Christ	0-87083-020-1
Gospel Outlines	0-87083-039-2
Character	0-87083-322-7
The Secret of Experiencing Christ	0-87083-227-1
The Life and Way for the Practice of the Church Life	0-87083-785-0
The Basic Revelation in the Holy Scriptures	0-87083-105-4
The Crucial Revelation of Life in the Scriptures	0-87083-372-3
The Spirit with Our Spirit	0-87083-798-2
Christ as the Reality	0-87083-047-3
The Central Line of the Divine Revelation	0-87083-960-8
The Full Knowledge of the Word of God	0-87083-289-1
Watchman Nee—A Seer of the Divine Revelation ...	0-87083-625-0

Titles by Watchman Nee:

How to Study the Bible	0-7363-0407-X
God's Overcomers	0-7363-0433-9
The New Covenant	0-7363-0088-0
The Spiritual Man 3 volumes	0-7363-0269-7
Authority and Submission	0-7363-0185-2
The Overcoming Life	1-57593-817-0
The Glorious Church	0-87083-745-1
The Prayer Ministry of the Church	0-87083-860-1
The Breaking of the Outer Man and the Release ...	1-57593-955-X
The Mystery of Christ	1-57593-954-1
The God of Abraham, Isaac, and Jacob	0-87083-932-2
The Song of Songs	0-87083-872-5
The Gospel of God 2 volumes	1-57593-953-3
The Normal Christian Church Life	0-87083-027-9
The Character of the Lord's Worker	1-57593-322-5
The Normal Christian Faith	0-87083-748-6
Watchman Nee's Testimony	0-87083-051-1

Available at

Christian bookstores, or contact Living Stream Ministry

2431 W. La Palma Ave. • Anaheim, CA 92801

1-800-549-5164 • www.livingstream.com